This Sacred Bond

A Pastoral Companion to *The Order of Celebrating Matrimony*

THE ORDER OF
CELEBRATING MATRIMONY

FDLC

Publications

ABBREVIATIONS:

AU	*Ad uxorem*, Tertullian (c. 200-205)
AA	*Apostolicam actuositatem* , Decree on the Apostolate of the Laity, Second Vatican Council, 1965
CCC	Catechism of the Catholic Church, *Libreria Editrice Vaticana*, 1997
CIC	*Codex Iuris Canonici*, Code of Canon Law, 1983
EG	*Evangelii Gaudium, The Joy of the Gospel*, Pope Francis, 2013
FC	*Familiaris consortio, Apostolic Exhortation*, Saint John Paul II, 1981
GS	*Gaudium et Spes*, Second Vatican Council, 1965
GIRM	*General Instruction of the Roman Missal*, United States Conference of Catholic Bishops, 2011
HV	*Humanae Vitae*, Blessed Pope Paul VI, 1968
LMI	*Lectionary for Mass: Introduction*, United States Conference of Catholic Bishops, 1998
LCDC	*Liturgy in a Culturally Diverse Community*, Federation of Diocesan Liturgical Commissions, 2012
LG	*Lumen Gentium*, Second Vatican Council, 1964
OCM	*Order of Celebrating Matrimony*, United States Conference of Catholic Bishops, 2016
PR	*Parish Ritual, (Collectio Rituum/ Rituale Romanum)* Benzinger Brothers, 1962
RM	*Rite of Marriage*, United States Conference of Catholic Bishops, 1970
RDM	*Ritual del Matrimonio*, Conferencia de Obispos Catolicos de los Estados Unidos, 2010
SC	*Sacrosanctum Concilium*, Second Vatican Council, 1963
SCAP	*Sunday Celebrations in the Absence of a Priest*, United States Conference of Catholic Bishops, 2007
SL	*Sing to the Lord: Music in Divine Worship*, United States Conference of Catholic Bishops, 2007

Contents

Introduction

THIS PASTORAL COMPANION: ITS PERSPECTIVE AND ITS PURPOSE

The Church values the matrimonial covenant between a husband and wife as a "lifelong partnership … [which] derives its force and strength from creation" (OCM 1). She sees the man and woman as an extension of the Creator's love for humanity. "Further, the institution of Marriage itself and conjugal love are, by their very nature, ordered to the procreation … of children" (OCM 3). "This sacred bond, therefore, does not depend on human choice, but rather on the Author of Marriage …" (OCM 4).

Matrimony, then, must be viewed through the lenses of theology and ecclesiology. It is a sacrament, an encounter with the Living God and a sign of Christ's saving presence among us. Like all sacraments, Matrimony not only expresses faith, but also constantly fosters a life deeply influenced by Christ and his Gospel.

True to her mission, the Church asks us to prepare couples to enter into marriage with a deep appreciation of the holiness of their vocation. This sacred bond cannot be entered into lightly. The Church — indeed, all members of the Church — should see it as their duty to nurture engaged couples, husbands, wives, and their families throughout this lifelong commitment.

The Church's understanding of Matrimony exists alongside many other societal viewpoints. Some cultural forces only see marriage as a contract between consenting adults; permanent as ideal, but temporary, if desired. These viewpoints also impact how one celebrates a wedding. Some will view the wedding celebration as a great reunion of family and friends. Some will want to travel to exotic places. Some will consider the celebration of marriage from the perspective of beginning a new family, deepening a loving relationship, and creating a happy home. Others consider a wedding from a monetary perspective — thinking of the cost of the wedding, catering, flowers, dresses, suits, and other purchases. Still others may stress about marriage preparation, judging it as a list of tasks to be done — managing countless details, balancing competing agendas, and allocating time, energy and attention. All of these viewpoints can affect how a couple approaches "being married."

The purpose of this Pastoral Companion is to help all of us who minister to engaged couples and married couples to see marriage, once again and still, for the holy vocation that it is. To do that, we will draw primarily from *The Order of Celebrating Matrimony* itself. There is an ancient expression within the Church's liturgical tradition — *lex orandi, lex credendi*. That is, "the law of praying is the law of believing." We don't pray anything that we don't believe and our beliefs reflect what we pray. The carefully chosen texts which we use in our worship, especially in our Mass and sacramental rites, are an expression of what we believe in faith.

The following pages, then, will examine the rite itself — its *praenotanda* (introductory notes), its rubrics, its dialogues, and its rich prayers. In this manner, we will attempt to plumb the riches of the theology they contain. This, in turn, will help us to better celebrate the Liturgy and to better serve those whose lives will be joined by this sacrament.

PART I

About *The Order of Celebrating Matrimony, Second Edition*

CHAPTER ONE: Examining *The Order Of Celebrating Matrimony, Second Edition*

A BRIEF HISTORY OF THE RITE

The Bishops of the Second Vatican Council called for the revision of the liturgical books, including the *Roman Ritual* — the collection of texts for the rites of the Church. Among these was a mandate to revise the Rite of Marriage. "The marriage rite now found in the Roman Ritual is to be revised and enriched in such a way that it more clearly signifies the grace of the sacrament and imparts a knowledge of the obligation of the spouses ..." (*Sacrosanctum Concilium: Constitution on the Sacred Liturgy*, no. 77, December 4, 1963).

The first typical edition of the *Ordo Celebrandi Matrimonium* was promulgated in Latin on March 19, 1969. Pope Paul VI ordered that its use was mandatory on July 1 of that year. Subsequently, the English translation of the *Rite for Celebrating Marriage* was published by the authority of the National Conference of Catholic Bishops in August 1970.

A second typical edition, *Ordo Celebrandi Matrimonium, editio typica altera*, was next promulgated by Saint John Paul II in 1990. This new edition had "an enrichment of the Introduction, rites and prayers, and with certain changes introduced in keeping with the norm of the Code of Canon Law promulgated in 1983" (Decree of Promulgation, Eduardo Cardinal Martinez, Prefect of the Congregation for Divine Worship and Discipline of the Sacraments, March 19, 1990). This Latin typical edition came into force immediately upon its publication, but with changes to the rules of translation and with priority given to other liturgical texts, including the Roman Missal, it took a few decades for this edition to be translated.

The Latin Rite Bishops of the United States approved a Spanish-language translation of this second edition in 2005. The provisional text was sent to the Congregation for Divine Worship and the Discipline of the Sacraments for the *recognitio* which is required before any new liturgical text can be published and used in the dioceses of the United States. That *recognitio* was received in 2008. In 2010, the *Ritual del Matrimonio* was published for use in the dioceses of the United States.

The Latin Rite Bishops of the USCCB approved the English translation of *The Order of Celebrating Matrimony, second edition* on November 12, 2013. Similarly, a recognitio was requested and it was granted on June 29, 2015. It is typical that a few months of "fine-tuning" of the text would follow, with a close examination of grammar and punctuation.

On February 2, 2016, Archbishop Joseph Kurtz, president of the USCCB, issued a Decree of Publication for *The Order of Celebrating Matrimony*. He wrote that this ritual text "may be published and used in the Liturgy as of September 8, 2016, the Feast of the Nativity of the Blessed Virgin Mary, and its use is mandatory as of December 30, 2016, the Feast of the Holy Family of Jesus, Mary, and Joseph. From that day forward, no other English edition of the *Order of Celebrating Matrimony* may be used in the dioceses of the United States."

Within the pages of this Pastoral Companion, we will explore this new English translation in detail.

The Order of Celebrating Matrimony, Second Edition

- Decrees
- Introduction
- Chapter I: The Order of Celebrating Matrimony within Mass
- Chapter II: The Order of Celebrating Matrimony without Mass
- Chapter III: The Order of Celebrating Matrimony between a Catholic and a Catechumen or a Non-Christian
- Chapter IV: Various Texts to Be Used in the Rite of Marriage and in the Mass for the Celebration of Marriage
- Appendices
    - Examples of the Universal Prayer
    - The Order of Blessing an Engaged Couple
    - The Order of Blessing a Married Couple within Mass on the Anniversary of Marriage

AN OVERVIEW OF THE CONTENTS

Like all liturgical texts, the front matter of the book begins with the official decrees which establish the rite's authority. These also provide a fascinating glimpse into who wrote the text, by whom it was promulgated, and when each edition was released. Moreover, these decrees provide insight into the process of revision, translation, and ecclesial authority. All this assures the "unbroken tradition" of the Church's liturgical texts and the rich theology which they express.

The decrees are followed by an Introduction (or *praenotanda*). The Introduction in the 1991 editions (and its 2016 English translation) has been greatly expanded — it now contains forty-four paragraphs as compared to eighteen in the 1969 edition. This book will examine these paragraphs, in detail, in Chapter 2.

The Introduction is followed by three chapters — each presents the ritual text for the three distinct, official rites which may be used when a Catholic marries. Each addresses a particular pastoral circumstance:

Chapter One:	The Order of Celebrating Matrimony within Mass
Chapter Two:	The Order of Celebrating Matrimony without Mass
Chapter Three:	The Order of Celebrating Matrimony between a Catholic and a Catechumen or a Non-Christian.

Chapter Four provides "Various Texts to Be Used in the Rite of Marriage and in the Mass for the Celebration of Marriage." These are divided into nine categories:

I.   Biblical Readings
        Readings from the Old Testament
        Readings from the New Testament
        Responsorial Psalms
        Alleluia Verses and Verses before the Gospel
        Gospel Readings
II.   Collects
III.   Other Prayers for the Blessing of Rings
IV.   Prayers over the Offerings
V.   Prefaces
VI.   Commemoration of the Couple in the Eucharistic Prayer
VII.   Other Prayers of Nuptial Blessing
VIII.   Prayers after Communion
IX.   Blessings at the End of the Celebration

Finally, the Appendices in the 2016 edition provide some very helpful prayers for use in a parish setting:

a)   Examples of the Universal Prayer (with two sets of sample invitations, petitions, and concluding prayers);
b)   The Order of Blessing an Engaged Couple (adapted from the *Book of Blessings*, Chapter I); and
c)   The Order of Blessing a Married Couple within Mass on the Anniversary of Marriage (adapted from the *Book of Blessings*, Chapter I, Part III-A).

WHAT REMAINS THE SAME?

When a revised rite is received, naturally questions center about what may have changed and what remains the same. In observing what remains unchanged, we note the following:

IN GENERAL

- The Introduction still speaks eloquently of the Church's earnest desire to promote the vocation of Marriage and to assist a man and a woman to prepare for married life.
- The basic structure for the *Rite of Marriage* as found in the 1969 edition remains — three rites for a Catholic's wedding in various pastoral circumstances. However, there are now expanded pastoral explanations on when to choose each rite.
- When two Catholics marry the preferred choice for *The Order of Celebrating Matrimony* remains a celebration within a Eucharistic Liturgy.
- The rite appropriately draws from and refers to the orations for the Ritual Mass. These are found in *The Roman Missal*, Ritual Mass V: "For the Celebration of Marriage."
- The essential elements of the rite remain the same — The Liturgy of the Word, the Consent, the Nuptial Blessing and Eucharistic Communion.

"The main elements of the celebration of Marriage are to stand out clearly, namely: The Liturgy of the Word, in which are expressed the importance of Christian Marriage in the history of salvation and the responsibilities and duties of Marriage to be attended to for the sanctification of the spouses and of their children; the consent of the contracting parties, which the person assisting asks for and receives; the venerable prayer by which the blessing of God is invoked upon the bride and bridegroom; finally, Eucharistic Communion of both spouses and of others present, by which, above all, their charity is nurtured and they are raised up to communion with the Lord and with their neighbor" (OCM 35).

- There are still two options for the greeting of the couple and the procession within the *Introductory Rites*. As before, there is no intent to spotlight the bride alone. The Congregation observed that various countries have different practices for the entrance procession, and so the rubric now states, "The procession to the altar then takes place in the customary manner" (OCM 46).
- There are still multiple options for readings from the *Lectionary* (OCM 33-35).
- The couple's Consent remains mostly unchanged, though some phrases have been changed. The rite still provides two options for the vows and two styles of expression (declarative and interrogatory). That is, they may be spoken by the bride and groom as a declarative sentence or spoken by the presider as a question, followed by the bride and groom's "I do."
- There are still options for the text of the *Nuptial Blessing*, but with stronger language to indicate that it may not be omitted in Rites I and II.

WHAT'S NEW?

IN GENERAL

- Parts of the Mass, especially the dialogues, acclamations, proper prayers and prefaces have been revised to conform with *The Roman Missal, third edition*.
- The translation of the entire text has followed the principles of translation as found in *Liturgiam Authenticam* (2001).
- The Ordinary of the Mass was printed in the 1969 edition. It does not appear in *The Order of Celebrating Matrimony, second edition*. It assumes the presider is using the Roman Missal. Some proper orations are reprinted in the OCM, Chapter IV.
- The revised *The Order of Celebrating Matrimony* includes an expanded Introduction. It has four main sections: "The Importance and Dignity of the Sacrament of Matrimony" (OCM 1-11); "Duties and Ministries" (12-27); "The Celebration of Matrimony" (28-38); and "Adaptations to be Prepared by the Conference of Bishops" (39-44).
- The text specifically refers to one man and one woman (OCM 1, 2).
- There is greater emphasis on the assembly, consistent with the expectation that the parish community shares in the ministry of Marriage (cf. OCM 12).
- The term "Matrimony" now appears in the title of the rite(s) and is used in reference to the sacrament. The term "Marriage" is used throughout in reference to the state of marriage.
- There are some new titles for the elements within the rites. For example, "The Exchange of Rings" now is more accurately titled "The Blessing and Giving of Rings."

MINISTERS

- While the 1969 Introduction did make reference to the duties of priests (RM 5, 7), the expanded Introduction has a new section entitled "Duties and Ministries." It begins with the responsibilities of the Bishop. It also delineates the duties of Priests, Deacons, and "the entire ecclesial community" (OCM 12).
- There is an expected relationship between the one who presides over the rite and the engaged couple. The OCM notes: "…the same Priest who prepares the couple should … give the Homily, receive the spouses' consent, and celebrate the Mass" (OCM 23).
- The 1969 edition of the OCM made no mention of Deacons. In the revised rite, a Deacon may preside at *The Order of Celebrating Matrimony without Mass* and *The Order of Celebrating Matrimony between a Catholic and a Catechumen or a Non-Christian* if he has been given the faculty to do so from the pastor or local Ordinary (OCM 24). A Deacon may not receive the vows of a couple during *The Order of Celebrating Matrimony within Mass* unless permission of the local Bishop has been obtained.
- The text provides specific directives regarding vesture for a Priest and a Deacon (OCM 45).

THE INTRODUCTORY RITES

- The instruction regarding how the entrance procession takes place is less specific and allows for a procession "in the customary manner" (OCM 46). The language about the bride and groom, witnesses and parents following the priest and other ministers has completely disappeared from the new English text. (However, it was retained in the Spanish text approved for use in the United States.)
- After the *Sign of the Cross and Greeting*, the revised edition now provides two choices for an introductory address by the minister. The first is addressed to the liturgical assembly; the second is addressed to the couple (OCM 52, 53).
- There is an explicit instruction that the *Penitential Act* is to be omitted.
- Respecting the directives in the third edition of the *Roman Missal*, the *Gloria* is now sung or said at Ritual Masses, even on weekdays of Lent and Advent.
- In the 1969 edition, there were four options for the Collect. Now there are six options, new or newly translated (OCM 188-193). These also appear in *The Roman Missal, third edition* in the propers for Ritual Mass V.

THE LITURGY OF THE WORD

- In Chapter One, a set of readings in provided, in place, within the text: Genesis 1:26-28,31a; Psalm 128:1-2,3,4-5ac,6a; Ephesians 5:2a,25-32; Alleluia with Psalm 134:3 or a Lenten acclamation (Psalm 81:2); and Matthew 19:3-6.
- In harmony with the *Lectionary for Mass*, the 2016 English translation provides nine Old Testament readings (eight were listed in the 1969 edition) and fourteen new Testament readings (ten were provided in the 1969 edition).
- The full text of each Scripture option is offered in Chapter Four.

THE CELEBRATION OF MARRIAGE

- Like the 1969 rite, there is an alternative formula for the Consent; it is based on the Sarum Rite (commonly used in other English-speaking countries and widely used in the Book of Common Prayer). To be consistent with other English speaking countries, the phrase, "to love and to cherish," has been added to form B.
- Both options for Consent still appear in both declarative and interrogatory forms. In the latter, the bride and groom simply state, "I do."

- The presider now has two options for the Reception of the Consent. The second is rich in biblical imagery.
- An acclamation praising God now follows the Reception of Consent: "*Let us bless the Lord/ Thanks be to God.*" Another acclamation may be sung or said in its place (OCM 65, 99, 130).
- Two optional, cultural adaptations have been included in the edition for the dioceses of the United States. These are ideally used in those liturgies where it is a familiar custom of the bride or groom's family. (However, there is nothing prohibiting their use by other couples.)
- These adaptations are the Blessing and Giving of the *Arras* (OCM 67B, 101B) and the Blessing and Placement of the *Lazo* (Lasso) or Veil (OCM 71B, 103B). The first occurs immediately after the Blessing and Giving of Rings. The couple exchange coins as a recognition of God's blessing and a sign of good gifts to be shared. The second option, the Blessing and Placing of the *Lazo* or the Veil, may take place before the Nuptial Blessing. Family and friends place a beaded cord or garland of flowers around the couple's shoulders; this may be accompanied by (or replaced by) a veil. Prayers for these options are included, in place, within the text.

THE LITURGY OF THE EUCHARIST

- Previously, a *Commemoration of the Couple* was provided for inclusion in Eucharistic Prayer I (Roman Canon). The new edition also provides an embolism for Eucharistic Prayers II and III (OCM 71 A, 202-204).
- New translations of the three Nuptial Blessings have been available in *The Roman Missal* since 2011. They have been included in the new edition of *The Order of Celebrating Matrimony*.
- The OCM has now added chant notation to encourage the presider to sing the Nuptial Blessing (OCM 205-209).
- The revised OCM clarifies that the Nuptial Blessing is never to be omitted. When pastoral circumstances warrant it, however, it may be omitted in *The Order of Celebrating Marriage Between a Catholic and a Catechumen or a Non-Christian*; in that case, another prayer is provided (OCM 138-140).
- A more generous permission is given for Holy Communion under both kinds (OCM 38, 76). The previous edition of the rite spoke only of Holy Communion under both kinds for the bride and groom.
- In *The Order of Celebrating Matrimony without Mass*, a full order of service is provided. A slightly alternative order is provided if Holy Communion is to be distributed. For very practical reasons, the full text of the Communion Rite is included (see OCM 108 ff.).

THE CONCLUSION OF THE CELEBRATION

- Three forms of the Solemn Blessing are provided. Form D of the Solemn Blessing, a USA Adaptation to the 1970 translation, has been eliminated in the 2016 edition.
- In each of the three rites, a new rubric appears about the signing of the marriage record.

THE APPENDIX

- The 1969 *Rite of Marriage* included two items in the Appendix — "Instructions on Communion under Both Kinds (as drawn from the 1969 edition of *The Roman Missal*) and extensive "Homiletic Notes for the New Readings" which offered pastoral commentary on the then newly-prescribed Scripture readings.
- Now the Appendix contains three helpful resources —
  1) Examples of the Universal Prayer; 2) The Order of Blessing an Engaged Couple; and 3) The Order of Blessing a Married Couple within Mass on the Anniversary of Marriage.

CHAPTER TWO: The Introduction to *The Order Of Celebrating Matrimony*

THE INTRODUCTION (OR *PRAENOTANDA*)

The best way to know and appreciate the Catholic Church's teachings regarding a sacrament is to read the introductory notes to its liturgical books. These are labeled as an "Introduction" or, in Latin, "*praenotanda*." While the Introduction to any liturgical text always contains practical guidelines for the celebration, it always begins with theology — what the Church believes about the nature of the sacrament, its meaning for our lives, and its place in the life of the Church.

In the second edition of *The Order of Celebrating Matrimony* (OCM), the Introduction has been expanded — from eighteen paragraphs in 1969, to forty-four paragraphs in 1991 (and its 2016 English translation). It draws upon the sacramental tradition of Matrimony within the Church, making specific reference to earlier Church documents. There are ten footnoted references to *Gaudium et Spes* (*The Pastoral Constitution on the Church in the Modern World*), five references to Pope John Paul II's Apostolic Exhortation, *Familiaris consortio*, eight references to *Sacrosanctum Concilium* (*Constitution on the Sacred Liturgy*), two references to *Lumen Gentium* (*Dogmatic Constitution on the Church*), numerous citations from New Testament Scripture, and references to the *Code of Canon Law*. There is one reference to *Apostolicam actuositatem* (*Decree on the Apostolate of the Laity*), and one to *Tertullian's Ad uxorem*. Clearly, our liturgical texts always build upon a rich tradition of magisterial teaching and maintain a consistency in the Church's theology and practice.

Building upon these insights, the Introduction speaks of the Church's understanding of the marital covenant between a man and a woman — its meaning to each of them, its power within society, and its importance within the Church.

The Introduction contains rich fodder for homilies. It also provides insights for parish preparation programs for engaged couples. Therefore, it is important to be familiar with its contents. The following will examine more closely the four parts of the Introduction to *The Order of Celebrating Matrimony*.

PART ONE: THE IMPORTANCE AND DIGNITY OF THE SACRAMENT OF MATRIMONY (OCM 1-11)

The first section of the newly-expanded Introduction offers a profound theology of the Sacrament of Matrimony and provides a summary of the fruits of the sacrament. This section, in particular, contains wonderful homiletic material.

1. The matrimonial covenant, by which a man and a woman establish a lifelong partnership between themselves,[1] derives its force and strength from creation, but for the Christian faithful it is also raised up to a higher dignity, since it is numbered among the Sacraments of the new covenant.
2. A Marriage is established by the conjugal covenant, that is, the irrevocable consent of both spouses, by which they freely give themselves to each other and accept each other. Moreover, this singular union of a man and a woman requires, and the good of the children demands, the complete fidelity of the spouses and the indissoluble unity of the bond.[2]
3. Furthermore, the institution ofMarriage itself and conjugal love are, by their very nature, ordered to the procreation and formation of children and find in them, as it were, their ultimate crown.[3] Children are thus truly the supreme gift of Marriage and contribute greatly to the good of the parents themselves.

4. The intimate community of life and love, by which spouses "are no longer two, but one flesh,"[4] has been established by God the Creator, provided with its own proper laws, and endowed with that blessing which alone was not forfeited by punishment for original sin.[5] This sacred bond, therefore, does not depend on human choice, but rather on the Author of Marriage, who ordained it be endowed with its own goods and ends.[6]

5. Indeed Christ the Lord, making a new creation and making all things new,[7] has willed that Marriage be restored to its primordial form and holiness in such a way that what God has joined together, no one may put asunder,[8] and raised this indissoluble conjugal contract to the dignity of a Sacrament so that it might signify more clearly and represent more easily the model of his own nuptial covenant with the Church.[9]

6. By his presence, Christ brought blessing and joy to the wedding at Cana, where he changed water into wine and so foreshadowed the hour of the new and eternal covenant: "For just as of old God made himself present to his people with a covenant of love and fidelity, so now the Savior of the human race"[10] offers himself to the Church as Spouse, fulfilling his covenant with her in his Paschal Mystery.

7. Through Baptism, which is the Sacrament of faith, a man and a woman are once and for all incorporated into the covenant of Christ with the Church in such a way that their conjugal community is assumed into Christ's charity and is enriched by the power of his Sacrifice.[11] From this new condition it follows that a valid Marriage between the baptized is always a Sacrament.[12]

8. By the Sacrament of Matrimony Christian spouses signify and participate in the mystery of unity and fruitful love between Christ and the Church;[13] therefore, both in embracing conjugal life and in accepting and educating their children, they help one another to become holy and have their own place and particular gift among the People of God.[14]

9. Through this Sacrament the Holy Spirit brings it about that, just as Christ loved the Church and gave himself up for her,[15] Christian spouses also strive to nurture and foster their union in equal dignity, mutual giving, and the undivided love that flows from the divine font of charity. In this way, uniting divine and human realities, they persevere in good times and in bad, faithful in body and mind,[16] remaining complete strangers to any adultery and divorce.[17]

10. The true development of conjugal love and the whole meaning of family life, without diminishment of the other ends of Marriage, are directed to disposing Christian spouses to cooperate wholeheartedly with the love of the Creator and Savior, who through them increases and enriches his family from day to day.[18] Therefore, trusting in divine Providence and developing a spirit of sacrifice,[19] they glorify the Creator and strive for perfection in Christ, as they carry out the role of procreation with generous, human and Christian responsibility.[20]

11. For God, who has called the couple to Marriage, continues to call them to Marriage.[21] Those who marry in Christ are able, with faith in the Word of God, to celebrate fruitfully the mystery of the union of Christ and the Church, to live it rightly, and to bear witness to it publicly before all. A Marriage that is desired, prepared for, celebrated, and lived daily in the light of faith is that which is "joined by the Church, strengthened by a sacrificial offering, sealed by a blessing, announced by Angels, and ratified by the Father. ... How wonderful the bond of the two believers: one in hope, one in vow, one in discipline, one in the same service! They are both children of one Father and servants of the same Master, with no separation of spirit and flesh. Indeed, they are two in one flesh; where there is one flesh, there is also one spirit."[22]

A BRIEF COMMENTARY ON PART ONE

Matrimony is a partnership with one's spouse for the whole of life. It is a conjugal covenant. A man and woman make an irrevocable consent to one another in the presence of the Church, and they make that consent before God. While a man and a woman are drawn to one another through love, it is the Creator who calls the couple to Marriage (OCM 4).

The Introduction affirms that the institution of Marriage "derives its force and strength from creation, but for the Christian faithful it is also raised to a higher dignity, since it is numbered among the Sacraments of the new covenant" (OCM 1, quoting CIC 1055.1).

Further, it speaks of the "irrevocable consent of both spouses, by which they freely give themselves to each other and accept each other ... this singular union of a man and a woman requires ... the complete fidelity of the spouses and the indissoluble unity of the bond" (OCM 2). Here, the Introduction affirms what was taught in Vatican II's *Pastoral Constitution on the Church in the Modern World: Gaudium et spes:*

> The intimate partnership of life and the love which constitutes the married state has been established by the creator and endowed by him with its own proper laws: it is rooted in the contract of its partners, that is, in their irrevocable personal consent. It is an institution confirmed by the divine law and receiving its stability, even in the eyes of society, from the human act by which the partners mutually surrender themselves to each other; for the good of the partners, of the children, and of society this sacred bond no longer depends on human decision alone. For God himself is the author of marriage and has endowed it with various benefits and with various ends in view: all of these have a very important bearing on the continuation of the human race, on the personal development and eternal destiny of every member of the family, on the dignity, stability, peace and prosperity of the family and of the whole human race. By its very nature the institution of marriage and married love is ordered to the procreation and education of the offspring and it is in them that it finds it crowning glory. Thus, the man and women, who "are no longer two by one (Mt. 19:6) help and serve each other by the marriage partnership; they become conscious of their unity and experience it more deeply from day to day. The intimate union of marriage, as a mutual giving of two persons, and the good of the children demand total fidelity from the spouses and require an unbreakable unity between them (GS 48).

"... Marriage and conjugal love are, by their very nature, ordered to the procreation and formation of children ... Children are thus truly the supreme gift of Marriage and contribute greatly to the good of the parents themselves" (OCM 3).

THE HOLINESS OF THE MARRIAGE COVENANT

The Introduction then affirms that Christ abundantly blesses this conjugal love which is rich in its attributes, springing from divine love and modeled on Christ's own union with the Church (OCM 4-5, GS 48). The mind of the Church prophetically places Marriage beyond the boundaries of a human decision. Marriage cannot be confined to a society's momentary understanding of what Marriage means at a particular time in history; rather, the Author of Marriage is God, who has always endowed Marriage with special benefits and purposes. In other words, what is celebrated is greater than only one couple's unique love.

The Church celebrates each new covenant of love and fidelity through the lens of the Paschal Mystery — the suffering, Death, Resurrection and Ascension of Jesus Christ — which will be lived out through the unique love of every Christian married couple (OCM 6).

> Just as of old God encountered his people with a covenant of love and fidelity, so our Savior, the spouse of the Church, now encounters Christian spouses through the sacrament of marriage. He abides with them in order that by their mutual self-giving, spouses will love each other with enduring fidelity, as he loved the Church and delivered himself for it (GS 48).

FOR THE BAPTIZED, MARRIAGE IS A SACRAMENT

"Through Baptism, which is the Sacrament of faith, a man and a woman are once and for all incorporated into the covenant of Christ with the Church in such a way that their conjugal community is assumed into Christ's charity and is enriched by the power of his Sacrifice. From this new condition it follows that a valid Marriage between the baptized is always a Sacrament" (OCM 7).

The Code of Canon Law is referenced in this context:

> The matrimonial covenant, by which a man and woman establish between themselves a partnership of the whole of life, and which is ordered by its nature to the good of the spouses and the procreation and education of offspring has been raised by Christ the Lord to the dignity of a sacrament between the baptized (CIC 1055.1).

> For this reason, a valid matrimonial contract cannot exist between the baptized without it being by that fact a sacrament (Canon 1055.2).

Man and woman are incorporated by baptism into the covenant of Christ with the Church. A married couple lives out their baptismal calling through their union in the Sacrament of Marriage.

THE MYSTERY OF THE UNITY BETWEEN CHRIST AND THE CHURCH

"By the Sacrament of Matrimony Christian spouses signify and participate in the mystery of unity and fruitful love between Christ and the Church; therefore, both in embracing conjugal life and in accepting and educating their children, they help one another to become holy and have their own particular gift among the People of God" (OCM 8).

This idea is drawn from Ephesians 5:25, "Husbands, love your wives, even as Christ loved the church and handed himself over for her ..." A married couple bears witness to the love of Christ each day as they live out their vocation — and share that love with their families and community.

This same theology is found in *Lumen Gentium 11* and in First Corinthians:

> Christian spouses, in virtue of the sacrament of Matrimony, whereby they signify and partake of the mystery of that unity and fruitful love which exists between Christ and His Church, help each other to attain to holiness in their married life and in the rearing and education of their children. By reason of their state and rank in life they have their own special gift among the people of God. From the wedlock of Christians there comes the family, in which new citizens of human society are born, who by the grace of the Holy Spirit received in baptism are made children of God, thus perpetuating the people of God through the centuries. The family is, so to speak, the domestic church ... In it parents should, by their word and example, be the first preachers of the faith to their children; they should encourage them in the vocation which is proper to each of them, fostering with special care vocation to a sacred state (LG 11).

> Each one has his own gift from God (1 Cor 7:7a).

This belief strengthens the urgency of the Church's desire to prepare an engaged couple for the Sacrament of Matrimony, helping the couple to embrace their role as Christian parents while living out their married lives in holiness.

MARRIED LOVE IS HUMAN AND DIVINE

"Through this Sacrament the Holy Spirit brings it about that, just as Christ loved the Church and gave himself up for her, Christian spouses also strive to nurture and foster their union in equal dignity, mutual giving, and the undivided love that flows from the divine font of charity. In this way, uniting divine and human realities, they persevere in good times and in bad, faithful in body and mind, remaining complete strangers to any adultery and divorce" (OCM 9).

Rooted in the Word of God, spouses are invited to nourish and foster their matrimonial union. Across the cultures many people have had and currently have a high regard for true love between husbands and wives and surround this regard with worthy customs. The Church views married love as eminently human, as it is an "affection between two persons rooted in the will of God and it embraces the good of the whole person" (GS 49).

The Introduction stresses that Christian spouses nurture and foster their union "in equal dignity, mutual giving, and and undivided love" (OCM 9). Truly successful marriages reflect this. The husband and wives respect each other, support one another, act selflessly, and always place priority on the needs of their spouse. This love is increased and deepened by the very exercise of it. Couples, thus, remain faithful to each other in good times and in bad.

This love is also a sharing in divine love, having been "restored, perfected and elevated" by Christ (GS 49). Selfless, unconditional, abiding love is God-like. It brings together the human and the divine.

The Church clearly believes that true married love creates the whole structure of family life, and asks that couples cooperate courageously with the love of God the Creator, and with the Savior, who are at work in the couple's life and marriage. Couples are urged to see their marital union as a way of interpreting how God is at work in the world, within their own relationship and within the larger world. Their roles as husband or wife, father or mother are joined with a deep reverence for God's action, as they seek the grace needed to live day by day in hope (OCM 10).

GOD CONTINUES TO CALL A COUPLE TO THEIR VOCATION

Finally, the *praenotanda* stresses that God, who first called the couple to Marriage, continues to sustain them: "For God, who has called the couple to Marriage, continues to call them to Marriage" (OCM 11).

This same sentiment is found in Pope St. John Paul II's apostolic exhortation, *Familiaris consortio* (1982) and Pope Paul VI's *Humanae vitae* (1968).

> This revelation reaches its definitive fullness in the gift of love which the Word of God makes to humanity in assuming a human nature, and in the sacrifice which Jesus Christ makes of Himself on the Cross for His bride, the Church. In this sacrifice there is entirely revealed that plan which God has imprinted on the humanity of man and woman since their creation; the marriage of baptized persons thus becomes a real symbol of that new and eternal covenant sanctioned in the blood of Christ. The Spirit which the Lord pours forth gives a new heart, and renders man and woman capable of loving one another as Christ has loved us. Conjugal love reaches that fullness to which it is interiorly ordained, conjugal charity, which is the proper and specific way in which the spouses participate in and are called to live the very charity of Christ who gave Himself on the Cross (*Familiaris consortio*, 13).

> In humble obedience then to [the Church's] voice, let Christian husbands and wives be mindful of their vocation to the Christian life, a vocation which, deriving from their Baptism, has been confirmed anew and made more explicit by the Sacrament of Matrimony. For by this sacrament they are strengthened and, one might almost say, consecrated to the faithful fulfillment of their duties. Thus will they realize to the full their calling and bear witness as becomes them, to Christ before the world (HV 32). For the Lord has entrusted to them the task of making visible to men and women the holiness and joy of the law which united inseparably their love for one another and the cooperation they give to God's love, God who is the Author of human life (HV 25).

God is always acting first, inviting a response. Entrusting their lives to the direction of the Word of God, those who marry in Christ are able to deepen the mystery of the union of Christ and the Church through living their Marriage in fidelity, bearing good fruit through their public witness of how God is blessing their married love. This is a Marriage that is "desired, prepared for, celebrated, and lived daily in the light of faith" (OCM 11). As the Church father, Tertullian, wrote in the third century:

This is a marriage ... joined by the Church, strengthened by a sacrificial offering, sealed by a blessing, announced by Angels, and ratified by the Father ... How wonderful the bond of the two believers; one in hope, one in discipline, one in the same service! They are both children of one Father and servants of the same Master, with no separation of spirit and flesh. Indeed, they are two in one flesh; where there is one flesh, there is also one spirit (AU II, VIII, as quoted in OCM 11).

PART TWO: DUTIES AND MINISTRIES (OCM 12-27)

The second section focuses on the ministers of the Church and their roles and responsibilities in the preparation and celebration of Marriage. The vision is broad, the ministries are many. It examines the role of the Bishop, Priest, Deacon, Lay Minister, and the entire parish community. Drawing on Canon Law and sound pastoral practice, it offers details on providing for the couple's sacramental and spiritual preparation.

12. The preparation and celebration of Marriage, which above all concern the future spouses themselves and their families, belong, as regards pastoral and liturgical care, to the Bishop, to the pastor and his associates, and, at least to some degree, to the entire ecclesial community.[23]

13. It is for the Bishop, who is to take into account any norms or pastoral guidelines that may have been established by the Conference of Bishops regarding the preparation of engaged couples or the pastoral care of Marriage, to regulate the celebration and pastoral care of the Sacrament throughout the diocese by organizing assistance for the Christian faithful so that the state of Marriage may be preserved in a Christian spirit and advance in perfection.[24]

14. Pastors of souls must take care that in their own community this assistance is provided especially: 1) by preaching, by catechesis adapted to children, young people, and adults, and through means of social communication, so that the Christian faithful are instructed about the meaning of Christian Marriage and about the role of Christian spouses and parents; 2) by personal preparation for entering Marriage, so that those to be married are disposed to the holiness and duties of their new state; 3) by a fruitful liturgical celebration of Marriage, so that it becomes clear that the spouses signify and participate in the mystery of the unity and fruitful love between Christ and the Church; 4) by help offered to those who are married, so that, faithfully preserving and protecting the conjugal covenant, they daily come to lead a holier and fuller family life.[25]

15. Sufficient time is required for a suitable preparation for Marriage. Engaged couples should be made aware of this necessity in advance.

16. Led by the love of Christ, pastors are to welcome engaged couples and, above all, to foster and nourish their faith: for the Sacrament of Matrimony presupposes and demands faith.[26]

17. The engaged couple, having been reminded, if appropriate, of the fundamental elements of Christian doctrine mentioned above (nos. 1-11) should be given catechesis not only about the Church's teaching on Marriage and the family but also about the Sacrament and its rites, prayers, and readings, so that they may be able to celebrate it thoughtfully and fruitfully.

18. Catholics who have not yet received the Sacrament of Confirmation are to receive it to complete their Christian Initiation before they are admitted to Marriage if this can be done without grave inconvenience. It is recommended to the engaged couple that in preparation for the Sacrament of Matrimony they receive the Sacrament of Penance, if necessary, and that they approach the Most Holy Eucharist, especially within the celebration of Marriage itself.[27]

19. Before a Marriage is celebrated, it must be established that nothing stands in the way of its valid and licit celebration.[28]

20. In conducting the preparation, pastors, taking into account prevailing attitudes toward Marriage and the family, should endeavor to evangelize the couple's authentic and mutual love in the light of faith. Even the requirements of law for contracting a valid and licit Marriage can serve to promote a living faith and fruitful love between the couple, ordered toward establishing a Christian family.

21. But if every effort fails, and an engaged couple openly and expressly demonstrate that they reject what the Church intends when the Marriage of baptized persons is celebrated, the pastor of souls is not permitted to celebrate the Sacrament. Though reluctant, he must take note of the situation and convince those involved that, in these circumstances, it is not the Church, but they themselves, who prevent the celebration they are asking for.[29]

22. With regard to Marriage, it is by no means rare for special cases to arise: such as Marriage with a baptized non-Catholic, with a catechumen, with a person who is simply unbaptized, or even with a person who has explicitly rejected the Catholic faith. Those in charge of pastoral care should keep in mind the norms of the Church pertaining to these types of cases, and they should, if the occasion requires, have recourse to the competent authority.

23. It is appropriate that the same Priest who prepares the engaged couple should, during the celebration of the Sacrament itself, give the Homily, receive the spouses' consent, and celebrate the Mass.

24. It also pertains to a Deacon, after receiving the faculty from the pastor or from the local Ordinary, to preside at the celebration of the Sacrament,[30] without omitting the Nuptial Blessing.

25. Where there is a shortage of Priests and Deacons, the Diocesan Bishop can delegate laypersons to assist at Marriages, after a prior favorable vote of the Conference of Bishops and after the permission of the Apostolic See has been obtained. A suitable layperson is to be selected, who is capable of giving instruction to those preparing to be married and able to perform the Marriage liturgy properly.[31] The layperson asks for the consent of the spouses and receives it in the name of the Church.[32]

26. Other laypersons, however, can play a part in various ways both in the spiritual preparation of the engaged couple and in the celebration of the rite itself. Moreover, the entire Christian community should cooperate to bear witness to the faith and to be a sign to the world of Christ's love.

27. The Marriage is to be celebrated in the parish of one or other of the engaged persons, or elsewhere with the permission of the proper Ordinary or pastor.[33]

A COMMENTARY ON PART TWO: THE PASTORAL CONTEXT

The diocese and local parish takes the responsibility of creating a pathway in which a couple prepares for both the wedding day and their entire married life.

Ministering always begins with taking the person as he/she is. This is especially true with the sacrament of Matrimony when we encounter engaged couples who bring their own perspectives to what a wedding must be and what married life should be. For good or ill, society has conditioned the couple to certain norms and practices surrounding preparation for and celebration of Matrimony. Friends have influenced their thoughts and their relationship. Ideally, the engaged couple's families have modeled what it means to live in a loving relationship and to raise a Christian family. However, that is not always the case — many women and men will come to the Church with a history of broken homes, divorces, and even abuse. Some couples will even come with their own history of a painful, failed marriage. What engaged couples have seen and experienced is sometimes their only guidepost. Not everything they have known has provided an example of a true Christian sacramental union.

The engaged couple's hearts may be filled with many emotions: joy, hope, anxiety, doubt, longing, passion, excitement, fear, thanksgiving. They want words and rituals to help them express what they are feeling. They want "their day" to be personalized. They want their family and friends to feel welcomed and cared for. They want to follow "traditions," and some of those traditions are nebulous.

The bride and groom also want to experience their wedding day without too many distractions or complications, and with everyone getting to the reception more or less intact. They do not want to be embarrassed with mistakes. Engaged couples can be very distracted with all the pieces of the "day." For some, this is the first event they have ever planned of this size or nature. Details and deadlines can overwhelm them and their families.

Those in ministry who work with engaged couples also bring their own experiences and perspectives to a wedding. Church ministers may know the couple well or not at all. Regardless, these ministers will want to provide good pastoral care and offer sound liturgical advice.

Yet despite all these possible crosscurrents, one truth remains: the bride and groom are the ministers of the sacrament. In their exchange of consent, they convey the Sacrament of Matrimony upon each other. They are guided by the Priest or Deacon who presides over the rite and serves as a witness for the Church. Within the celebration of Matrimony the engaged couple have specific words which they must say to the Priest or Deacon, say to one another, and say to God. The presider and the entire liturgical assembly bear witness to this.

It is in this pastoral context that the Church and her ministers prepare an engaged couple both for the vocation of Matrimony and for the celebration of the wedding liturgy. This Sacrament, prepared for and celebrated well, will sustain the newly married couple for the many years. Their future may be filled with great joys and great sorrows, but it will always be sustained by God's grace.

In preparing for the wedding day, ministers may be conflicted by some requests from the engaged couple. They may be mystified by the rituals which a couple wants to add to the wedding ceremony. Difficult questions may be raised about modesty in dress for the wedding party, minimum age requirements of witnesses, or requests for music which does not speak of sacramental love. Ministers may be frustrated by people who seem to have little understanding of the rites of the Church. Frequently, there can be a tension between a request for personalization and the need to observe the rubrics of *The Order of Celebrating Matrimony*. However, it is always beneficial to include couples in the preparation of the rite, allowing them to choose among the options provided.

How do the Church ministers and the engaged couples find ways to integrate the perspectives they bring about Marriage and the wedding liturgy? Answering these questions can be a challenge for sure; yet, the answering, if done collaboratively with the presider and the couple, can produce a harvest of grace.

THE BISHOP

The diocesan Bishop, taking into account any norms or pastoral guidelines from the Conference of Bishops, has the responsibility to provide the means by which engaged couples can be prepared for Marriage. He regulates the celebration and the pastoral care of the Sacrament throughout the diocese. This means the Bishop will direct both clergy and laity in this diocesan effort, with specific programs for the engaged, usually coordinated at the diocesan level and experienced at the parish level. In this way, "the state of Marriage may be preserved in a Christian spirit and advance in perfection" (OCM 13).

In every diocese, "sufficient time is required for a suitable preparation for Marriage. Engaged couples should be made aware of this necessity in advance" (OCM 15).

PRIESTS

Besides the Bishop, the OCM addresses the specific duties of "pastors of souls." These are considered to be pastors of parishes and those priests who assist them. Pastors are to welcome engaged couples with charity, and are to foster and nourish the engaged couple's faith. Pastors promote Marriage as a vocation in many ways: preaching, catechesis for children and adults, the use of social communication, personal involvement in marriage preparation of engaged couples; fruitful preparation of the rite and celebrating it well, and helping married couples and families lead a holier life (cf. OCM 14).

Indeed, in the celebration of the wedding liturgy itself, "... it becomes clear that the spouses signify and participate in the Mystery of the unity and fruitful love between Christ and the Church ..." (*ibid*).

DEACONS

On June 18, 1967, Blessed Pope Paul VI issued an Apostolic Letter, *motu proprio*, *Sacrum Diaconatus Ordinem: General Norms for Restoring the Permanent Diaconate in the Latin Church*. In it, he gave permission to Conferences of Bishops to consider restoring the permanent diaconate within their territories. Since that document was not in full force in 1969, the previous edition of the *Rite of Marriage* did not mention Deacons when discussing Marriage preparation or the Marriage rite.

But the 1991 edition, drawing upon Canon 1111, specifically mentions the Deacon's role:

> It also pertains to a Deacon, after receiving the faculty from the pastor or from the local Ordinary, to preside at the celebration of the Sacrament, without omitting the Nuptial Blessing (OCM 24).

If they have been granted such faculties, Deacons may preside over Rites II and III — *The Order of Celebrating Matrimony without Mass* or *The Order of Celebrating Matrimony between a Catholic and a Catechumen or a Non-Christian*.

PRESIDERS

A presider leads the assembly in prayer, directs the actions of the other ministers, preaches on the Scriptures, and serves as the Church's official witness to the Consent exchanged by the couple. He demonstrates the Church's concern for the engaged couple by his pastoral care and attention to the proper celebration of the rite.

> It is appropriate that the same Priest who prepares the engaged couple should, during the celebration of the Sacrament itself, give the Homily, receive the spouse's consent and celebrate the Mass (OCM 23).

The mystery of the unity and fruitful love between Christ and the Church should be a significant aspect of leading the sacramental liturgy. The Priest or Deacon expresses the faith of the Church through words and rituals. Sometimes, even silence can convey the Mystery of God acting in human lives. The words of our rites are important and should never be set aside for words of one's own invention. Words which are trite, inappropriate, banal, or confusing cannot communicate the mystery. When rituals are ignored or trivialized, they fail to speak and "don't work" as intended. Every leader of prayer must appreciate how each liturgical rite uses words and actions. This necessitates learning the rich history behind them.

When a presider leads the entire assembly in prayer, is he aware of verbal and non-verbal communications? For example, does his posture and placement convey leadership? Does it engage the assembly? Is the presider attentive when the readings are proclaimed? Has appropriate and worthy vesture been chosen? Do vestments call attention to the presider or are they dignified and subdued? Do gestures and posture follow the rubrics in the liturgical books? Do they convey reverent prayer? How does eye contact, volume, pace, and articulation impact communication with the assembly?

LAY PRESIDERS

"When there is a shortage of Priests and Deacons, the Diocesan Bishop can delegate lay persons to assist at Marriages, after a prior favorable vote of the Conference of Bishops and after the permissions of the Apostolic See has been obtained. A suitable lay person is to be selected, who is capable of giving instruction to those preparing to be married and able to perform the Marriage liturgy properly. The layperson asks for the consent of the spouses and receives it in the name of the Church" (OCM 25; cf. Canon 1108.2 and Canon 1115). At this writing, this permission has not been sought for the dioceses of the United States.

THE PARISH MUSIC DIRECTOR

The parish Music Director will be an important part of this patient dialogue among the presider, future bride, and future groom. The pastoral musician has a twofold role. First, the musician serves as a resource to guide the engaged couple through the process of selecting and preparing music for their wedding. Second, the pastoral musician leads the music for the wedding liturgy itself.

> The chants to be sung during the Rite of Marriage should be appropriate and should express the faith of the Church, with attention paid to the importance of the Psalm within the Liturgy of the Word. What is said concerning the chants applies also to the selection of other musical works (OCM 30).

Elsewhere in this Pastoral Companion you will find a more extensive exploration of music at a Catholic wedding. (Please turn to page 98.)

OTHER LITURGICAL MINISTERS

Since *The Order of Celebrating Matrimony* is a liturgical rite, liturgical ministers should be prepared and qualified to serve. Couples will often want to choose family members or friends to serve as the Readers, Extraordinary Ministers of Holy Communion, Altar Servers, Ministers of Hospitality, or Music Ministers. Since each of these ministers must serve the liturgical assembly with competence, careful discussion might accompany the selection process. A well-prepared rehearsal will alleviate discomfort. The parish's regular liturgical ministers should also be willing to assist, when necessary, at wedding liturgies. (For more detailed information on liturgical ministers, please turn to page 40.)

THE LITURGICAL ASSEMBLY

All members of the assembly — liturgical ministers, bride, groom, parents, wedding party, family and friends — celebrate the wedding liturgy. Therefore, it is important that they participate in the prayer, spoken and sung. By its very nature, liturgy is dialogic and communal. Together, we worship the living God. Together, we pray for this bride and groom. Together, the Church prays with and for those not present, living and dead. The liturgical assembly is engaged in prayer that is specific to the liturgy, yet more expansive than the moment.

THE LOCAL PARISH

When seeking Marriage within the Church, the engaged couple first approaches the local parish. It may be their own "home parish" where they grew up or perhaps the parish near their university or new job.

In general, Marriage preparation focuses on catechetical formation about the Sacrament of Matrimony and married life. Through various processes an engaged couple is assisted in discerning their mature and free consent to enter into married life through the Sacrament of the Church. It should also include liturgical formation and the thoughtful preparation of the wedding liturgy. While a pastor can work with others in providing marriage preparation programs, he should have some part in personally working with couples, particularly in helping the engaged focus on their dispositions toward holiness and the duties of married life.

However, laypersons can play a vital role in the spiritual preparation of the couple and in the celebration of the rite itself. Married couples who lead engaged couples' weekends, mentor couples who walk with the engaged couple in private sessions, parish staff people who contribute to catechesis, parish musicians, other liturgical ministers, and wedding coordinators all can bear witness to their faith as they serve engaged couples.

Other laypersons ... can play a part in various ways both in the spiritual preparation of the engaged couple and the celebration of the rite itself. Moreover, the entire Christian Community should cooperate to bear witness to the faith and to be a sign to the world of Christ's love (OCM 26).

A local parish should be continually formed in an ongoing study of the meaning of Christian Marriage and the roles of Christian spouses and parents. This is crucial within a culture that may not value a Christian understanding of Marriage. This catechesis happens in a variety of ways — 1) Preaching on the Scriptures about the married life; 2) using means of social communication; 3) regular adult education sessions on marriage; and even fruitful discussions with the teens and young adults of the parish. In addition, the parish should create support systems for all married couples, including access to marriage counseling and spiritual direction when difficulties between husbands and wives arise.

PASTORAL CARE AND EVANGELIZATION

"Led by the love of Christ, pastors are to welcome engaged couples and, above all, to foster and nourish their faith: for the Sacrament of Matrimony presupposes and demands faith" (OCM 16). Evangelizing the couple is still a vital task for the Church's ministers.

> In conducting the preparation, pastors, taking into account prevailing attitudes toward Marriage and the family, should endeavor to evangelize the couple's authentic and mutual love in the light of faith. Even the requirements of law for contracting a valid and licit Marriage can serve to promote a living faith and fruitful love between the couple ordered toward establishing a Christian family (OCM 20).

The Order of Celebrating Matrimony, itself, seeks to help form a couple's understanding about the Sacrament of Matrimony in the same way the Church understands Matrimony. Thus, how the rite is celebrated is an integral part of this evangelization.

While there are many issues that must be determined while preparing for a wedding, the issues of Marriage suitability and a willingness by the engaged couple to be a part of the Church is a great responsibility. The Church understands this engagement time to be one where God is involved in human living. God's grace is given to the couple to live out this committed love. There is an expectation that an engaged couple be prepared through catechesis about the state of Marriage, the dynamics of family, and the spirit and practice of the liturgical celebrations.

For some couples this evangelization may mean understanding that this sacrament is yet another step in their baptismal journey. They understand that this sacrament, too, strengthens their faith through Christ and with each other.

On the other hand, for some couples, this is their first encounter with the Church in many years. One or both of the engaged may have been raised Roman Catholic with some degree of religious formation, while one or both may have little to no formal religious formation at all. The circle in which some couples move may have little to do with religious faith. Some may consider themselves "spiritual," but have no affiliation with any denomination. In whatever circumstances ministers meet an engaged couple, evangelization means bringing the Gospel of Jesus Christ into the conversation — looking for points of entry in which a couple can embrace Christ's Church as the way through which they express their relationship with each other and with Christ.

The first skill is listening. The second skill is patient teaching. Perhaps, the vocabulary may need explanation. Perhaps, the requirements of the Church may appear to some to be burdensome. Perhaps, the sense of the Church's celebration of Matrimony may need patient exploring so that the minister may enlighten the couple on what the Church hopes for the couple and their marriage. "*Engagement*" describes the couple's journey together prior to the wedding day. The word engagement also illustrates how the dialogue with the engaged couple and with those who minister in the name of the Church will produce good fruit moving them ever closer to Christ through the Church.

The revised Introduction goes into greater detail about the pastoral care offered to an engaged couple. Some paragraphs are totally new (nos. 18-27); some draw from paragraphs in the 1969 edition; and some elaborate on the 1983 *Code of Canon Law*.

For the Catholic bride and/or groom, the parish minister should examine their sacramental history. If they have not already received the Sacrament of Confirmation, they will be expected to receive it, if possible. They should also be encouraged to participate in the Sacrament of Reconciliation (Penance) and the frequent celebration of the Eucharist (OCM 18).

"Before Marriage is celebrated, it must be established that nothing stands in the way of its valid and licit celebration" (OCM 19). First and foremost, each person must be free to marry. If there are any previous marriages and the ex-spouse is still living, the marriage(s) must be annulled. The person must also be mentally capable of exchanging vows with another person. For a full treatment of significant canonical issues, please see the *Code of Canon Law*, canons 1063 to 1107.

Paragraph twenty-one raises a very serious pastoral issue. What happens when an engaged person or couple rejects what the Church intends when the marriage of baptized persons is celebrated? The pastor of souls is not permitted to celebrate the Sacrament under these circumstances. While this painful result should be a rare case, it does emphasize that the Church is serious about preparation and sacramental integrity. If a couple cannot enter willingly into what is offered to them by the Church, the couple bears the responsibility for that. This can be deeply alienating for the couple and their families, so every effort should be made by the Church to help catch the couple in the net of the Gospel.

RITES FOR PASTORAL CIRCUMSTANCES

Like most liturgical books, *The Order of Celebrating Matrimony* offers texts for various pastoral circumstances. All three rites are valid liturgies when a Catholic marries — when he/she marries another Catholic, marries a non-Catholic Christian, or marries a catechumen or one who is not baptized. Paragraph twenty-two mentions some exceptional or special cases. It reminds the presider about Church norms and the right to have recourse to competent authority.

PART THREE: THE CELEBRATION OF MATRIMONY (OCM 28-38)

Part Three offers prescriptions for the preparation of the liturgy (28-32) and the rite to be used (33-38)

28. Since Marriage is ordered toward the increase and sanctification of the People of God, its celebration displays a communitarian character that encourages the participation also of the parish community, at least through some of its members. With due regard for local customs and as occasion suggests, several Marriages may be celebrated at the same time or the celebration of the Sacrament may take place during the Sunday assembly.

29. The celebration itself of the Sacrament must be diligently prepared, as far as possible, with the engaged couple. Marriage should normally be celebrated within Mass. Nevertheless, with due regard both for the necessities of pastoral care and for the way in which the prospective spouses and those present participate in the life of the Church, the pastor should decide whether it would be preferable to propose that Marriage be celebrated within or outside of Mass.[34] The following should be chosen with the engaged couple, as the circumstances so suggest: the readings from Sacred Scripture, which will be explained in the Homily; the form for expressing mutual consent; the formularies for the blessing of rings, for the Nuptial Blessing, for the intentions of the Universal Prayer or Prayer of the Faithful, and for the chants. Moreover, attention should also be given to the appropriate use of options provided in the rite as well as to local customs, which may be observed if appropriate.

30. The chants to be sung during the Rite of Marriage should be appropriate and should express the faith of the Church, with attention paid to the importance of the Responsorial Psalm within the Liturgy of the Word. What is said concerning the chants applies also to the selection of other musical works.

31. The festive character of the celebration of Marriage should be suitably expressed even in the manner of decorating the church. Nevertheless, local Ordinaries are to be vigilant that, apart from the honors due to civil authorities in keeping with the norm of liturgical laws, no favoritism be shown to private persons or classes of persons.[35]

32. If a Marriage is celebrated on a day having a penitential character, especially during Lent, the pastor is to counsel the spouses to take into account the special nature of that day. The celebration of Marriage on Friday of the Passion of the Lord and Holy Saturday is to be avoided altogether.

33. In the celebration of Marriage within Mass, the rite described in Chapter I is used. In the celebration of Marriage without Mass, the rite should take place after a Liturgy of the Word according to the norm of Chapter II.

34. Whenever Marriage is celebrated within Mass, the Ritual Mass "The Celebration of Marriage" is used with sacred vestments of the color white or of a festive color. On those days listed in nos. 1-4 of the Table of Liturgical Days, however, the Mass of the day is used with its own readings, with inclusion of the Nuptial Blessing and, if appropriate, the proper formula for the final blessing.

    If, however, during Christmas and Ordinary Time, the parish community participates in a Sunday Mass during which Marriage is celebrated, the Mass of the Sunday is used.

    Nevertheless, since a Liturgy of the Word adapted for the celebration of Marriage has a great impact in the handing on of catechesis about the Sacrament itself and about the duties of the spouses, when the Mass "For the Celebration of Marriage" is not said, one of the readings may be taken from the texts provided for the celebration of Marriage (nos. 144-187).

35. The main elements of the celebration of Marriage are to stand out clearly, namely: the Liturgy of the Word, in which are expressed the importance of Christian Marriage in the history of salvation and the responsibilities and duties of Marriage to be attended to for the sanctification of the spouses and of their children; the consent of the contracting parties, which the person assisting asks for and receives; the venerable prayer by which the blessing of God is invoked upon the bride and bridegroom; finally, Eucharistic Communion of both spouses and of others present, by which, above all, their charity is nurtured and they are raised up to communion with the Lord and with their neighbor.[36]

36. If a Marriage takes place between a Catholic and a baptized non-Catholic, the rite for celebrating Matrimony without Mass (nos. 79-117) should be used. If, however, the situation warrants it, the rite for celebrating Matrimony within Mass (nos. 45-78) may be used, with the consent of the local Ordinary; but with regard to admission of the non-Catholic party to Eucharistic Communion, the norms issued for various cases are to be observed.[37] If a Marriage takes place between a Catholic and a catechumen or a non-Christian, the rite given below (nos. 118-143) is to be used, with the variations provided for different situations.

37. Although pastors are ministers of Christ's Gospel for all, they should, nonetheless, direct special attention to those, whether Catholics or non-Catholics, who never or rarely take part in the celebration of Marriage or the Eucharist. This pastoral norm applies in the first place to the spouses themselves.

38. If Marriage is celebrated within Mass, in addition to those things required for the celebration of Mass, *The Order of Celebrating Matrimony* and rings for the spouses should be prepared in the sanctuary. There should also be prepared, if appropriate, a vessel of holy water with an aspergillum and a chalice of sufficient size for Communion under both kinds.

The principles found in Part Three will be explored in great detail within the pages of this book, but a few introductory comments are provided below.

PREPARATION OF THE RITE

"Since Marriage is ordered toward the increase and sanctification of the People of God, its celebration displays a communitarian character that encourages the participation also of the parish community, at least through some of its members" (OCM 28). Thus, it is important to involve competent ministers in the preparation of the liturgy and to give the parish community a sense of supporting each engaged couple.

Presiders will want to encourage the involvement of the bride and groom in preparing the wedding liturgy. In particular, they might choose the readings from Sacred Scripture, the form of expressing the Consent (the vows), the formularies for the blessing of rings, the form of the Nuptial Blessing, the wording of the Universal Prayer (or Prayer of the Faithful), and the music (OCM 29).

The Introduction speaks of the importance of music in the celebration of the Marriage liturgy (30) and the festive nature of the celebration and the decoration of the church (31). It cautions against showing favoritism to any private persons or classes of person (OCM 31; see also SC 32). It also cautions about celebrations held on days of a penitential character. On these days the pastor should counsel the couple about the nature of the liturgical day. Indeed, the text prohibits the celebration of Marriage on Friday of the Passion of the Lord (Good Friday) or Holy Saturday (OCM 33).

THE RITE TO BE USED

Here, the Introduction gets into specific advice and legislation regarding the choice of rite. Much of this section is drawn from the 1969 edition of the *Rite of Marriage* (nos. 6, 8, 9, and 11), but new clarifications are helpful. The presider is directed to Chapter One for *The Order of Celebrating Matrimony within Mass* and to Chapter Two for *The Order of Celebrating Matrimony without Mass* (OCM 33).

When one chooses the Ritual Mass, "*For the Celebration of Marriage*," vesture is indicated (OCM 34). That same paragraph names those liturgical days on which Ritual Mass may not be used, then explains how the choice of readings and the inclusion of the Nuptial Blessing may alter the celebrations on these liturgical days. [For further information, please see pages 42-43.]

Paragraph thirty-five identifies the main elements of the wedding liturgy.

Paragraph thirty-six directs the presider to Chapter Two for the rite of Marriage between a Catholic and non-Catholic, but notes that the celebration may take place within Mass with permission of the local Ordinary, keeping in mind legislation about the admission to Eucharistic Communion. Next, the paragraph directs the presider to Chapter Three for the wedding of a Catholic and catechumen or a non-baptized person. Indeed, the language is quite clear — this rite "is to be used" (OCM 36) for the wedding of a Catholic and a non-baptized person.

The Introduction offers additional encouragement to pastors of souls on their duty to engage those who are unchurched and who are attending the wedding. "This pastoral norm applies in the first place to the spouses themselves" (OCM 37).

Finally, it notes requisites which must be prepared for Mass — including the ritual text, rings, holy water, "and a chalice of sufficient size for Communion under both kinds" (OCM 38).

Finally, Part Four details which adaptations may be made to this universal document, allowing Conferences of Bishops to adapt the Roman Ritual to the customs and needs of particular regions.

39. It is for the Conferences of Bishops, by virtue of the Constitution on the Sacred Liturgy,[38] to adapt this Roman Ritual to the customs and needs of the particular regions, so that, once their decisions have been accorded the *recognitio* of the Apostolic See, the edition may be used in the regions to which it pertains.

40. In this regard, it is for the Conferences of Bishops: 1) To formulate the adaptations indicated below (nos. 41-44); 2) If necessary, to adapt and supplement this Introduction of the Roman Ritual from no. 36 and what follows (in "The Rite to Be Used"), so as to achieve the conscious and active participation of the faithful; 3) To prepare versions of the texts, so that they are truly accommodated to the nature of different languages and the character of diverse cultures, and to add, whenever appropriate, suitable melodies for singing; 4) In preparing editions, to arrange the material in a form more suitable for pastoral use.

41. In preparing adaptations, the following points should be kept in mind: 1) The formulas of the Roman Ritual may be adapted and, if necessary, even supplemented (even the questions before the consent and the words of the consent themselves); 2) Whenever the Roman Ritual gives several optional formulas, it is permitted to add other formulas of the same kind; 3) Provided the structure of the sacramental rite is preserved, the order of the parts may be adapted. If it seems more appropriate, the questions before the consent may be omitted, provided the law is observed that the person assisting ask for and receive the consent of the contracting parties; 4) Should pastoral need so demand, it can be determined that the consent of the contracting parties always be sought by questioning; 5) After the giving of rings, in keeping with local customs, the crowning of the bride or the veiling of the spouses may take place; 6) Wherever the joining of hands or the blessing and giving of rings are incompatible with the culture of the people, it may be decided that these rites be omitted or replaced by other rites; 7) It should be carefully and prudently considered what elements from the traditions and culture of particular peoples may appropriately be adopted.

42. In addition, in accordance with the norm of the Constitution on the Sacred Liturgy (art. 63b), each Conference of Bishops has the faculty to draw up its own Marriage rite appropriate to the customs of the place and the people, with the decision approved by the Apostolic See, provided the law is observed that the person assisting must ask for and receive the consent of the contracting parties[39] and the Nuptial Blessing must be given.[40] The Introduction in the Roman Ritual is to be prefixed even to a proper ritual,[41] except for those points that refer to the rite to be used.

43. In the usages and ways of celebrating Marriage prevailing among peoples now receiving the Gospel for the first time, whatever is honorable and not indissolubly connected with superstition and errors should be sympathetically considered and, if possible, preserved intact, and in fact even admitted into the Liturgy itself as long as it harmonizes with a true and authentic liturgical spirit.[42]

44. Among peoples for whom the Marriage ceremonies customarily take place in homes, even over a period of several days, these ceremonies should be adapted to the Christian spirit and to the Liturgy. In this case the Conference of Bishops, in accordance with the pastoral needs of the people, may determine that the rite of the Sacrament itself can be celebrated in homes.

In *The Constitution on the Sacred Liturgy*, the Bishops of the Second Vatican Council called for the revision of all the liturgical books. They addressed the revision of the marriage rite in paragraph seventy-seven:

> The marriage rite now found in the Roman Ritual is to be revised and enriched in such a way that it more clearly signifies the grace of the sacrament and imparts the obligation of spouses.

> "If any regions follow other praiseworthy customs and ceremonies when celebrating the sacrament of marriage, the Council earnestly desires that by all means these be retained" (quoting the Council of Trent, Session One, *Decree on Reform*, chap. 1).

> Moreover, the competent, territorial ecclesiastical authority mentioned in art. 22, §2 of this Constitution is free to draw up, in accord with art. 63, its own rite, suited to the usages of place and people. But the rite must always conform to the law that the priest assisting at marriage must ask for and obtain the consent of the contracting parties.

The universal Church exists within a variety of cultures and recognizes many traditions. Not all marriage ceremonies are alike. The Church must use these rites effectively to advance the Gospel of Christ and to encourage the conscious and active participation of the faithful. They are permitted to prudently consider which elements from the traditions and culture of particular peoples may be appropriately adapted. There is wisdom in using language, customs, and rituals which speak to the people and which have been judged to harmonize with a true, authentic liturgical spirit.

The paragraphs in Part Four of the Introduction reiterate the rights and responsibilities of local Bishops' Conferences. They may propose adaptations to the *Roman Ritual*, based on the customs and needs of particular regions in the world (cf. SC 37-40, 63b,77).

First, the Introduction lists those things which the Conference of Bishops may change (OCM 40), including adaptations and supplements to the Introduction, suitable options and formulas, and melodies for singing. The Conference may also arrange the material in a form more suitable for pastoral use and publish it in various languages. The OCM also lists how elements are to be adapted (OCM 41). In addition, a conference may draw up its own rite (OCM 42), provided it retains important elements, especially the Consent of the couple. In mission territories, "among peoples now receiving the Gospel for the first time," local customs may be admitted to the Liturgy "as long as it harmonizes with a true and authentic liturgical spirit" (OCM 43). Finally, since this is a universal document, the Introduction speaks about the custom of weddings in homes (cf. OCM 44).

Any adaptations to a liturgical book are then sent to the Congregation for Divine Worship and Discipline of the Sacraments of the Apostolic See. The *Ordo Celebrandi Matrimonium, editio typica altera* is the result of such adaptation, collaboration, and consultation.

PART II

Preparing the Wedding Liturgy

CHAPTER THREE:
Principles for Preparing the Liturgy

PREPARATION OF THE ORDER OF CELEBRATING MATRIMONY

The preparation for Marriage includes the thoughtful and careful preparation of the wedding liturgy. One cannot attempt this without a firm understanding of the nature of liturgy and an acknowledgment of the basic principles of liturgical preparation.

THE NATURE OF LITURGY

Liturgy is the official communal worship of the Church. The words "official" and "communal" are equally important. The Liturgy of the Church is not created out of personal whims nor personal piety. Official liturgical texts are based on centuries of praxis and tradition. Words are carefully translated into countless languages from a single, universal source. The word "liturgy" comes from the Greek word *litourgia* — "the work of the people." It is not an action of a single person, but of a body of worshippers called together by God to give him due praise. Put another way, the liturgy is God's work and we are invited to participate in this work (CCC 1069).

The Constitution on the Sacred Liturgy defined the two purposes of Liturgy — "God's glorification and human sanctification" (SC 10). The end result is twofold — to praise God and to help us become more holy. Both of these ends are vital.

What basic principles, then, should guide our preparations and celebrations which have such noble goals?

LITURGY CELEBRATES THE PASCHAL MYSTERY

The Paschal Mystery refers to the Christian belief that the salvation of all humankind has been accomplished through Jesus Christ. It is through Jesus Christ's Passion, Death and Resurrection that our sins have been forgiven and our salvation has been won. We Christians celebrate what has already been accomplished by God in Christ. The focus or central theme of any liturgical celebration is the Paschal Mystery of Jesus Christ — with Christ, and through Christ, we are remembering and making present his saving actions. Throughout the ages, we continue to gather for liturgical celebrations — all liturgical celebrations — to call to mind once again and still, this great truth of our salvation. We never cease to give God thanks for so great a gift!

The Constitution on the Sacred Liturgy expresses it well:

> [Therefore] in Christ, the perfect achievement of our reconciliation came forth and the fullness of divine worship was given to us ... He achieved his task of redeeming humanity and giving perfect glory to God, principally by the paschal mystery of his blessed passion, resurrection from the dead , and glorious ascension, whereby "dying he destroyed our death and rising he restored our life." For it was from the side of Christ as he slept the sleep of death upon the cross that there came forth the sublime sacrament of the whole Church (SC 5).

The late liturgical scholar Mark Searle said that the Paschal Mystery was a *kind of a spiral* in which a person enters into an ever-deepening experience of this Mystery. That Mystery is encountered and expressed through Word and Sacrament, ritual and prayers, music and silence.

Through Christ and with his Church, we are preparing to celebrate the Sacrament of Matrimony. This couple, and all attending, have already been participating in this Paschal Mystery, and will do so within all time. God is present, active in the life of this engaged couple, and will walk with them in their married life yet to unfold. God will be faithful to them. He calls them to a holy life, and to the Kingdom of heaven, now and beyond death.

What might this mean to those planning a wedding liturgy? Sometimes we talk about a wedding as "the bride and groom's big day," as if it belongs to the bride and groom. This is often a strong cultural understanding. A great deal of work goes into this "big day," not only by the bride and groom but also both families and friends. In a sense, we are celebrating the couple's commitment to marry. But something greater is happening. The Church encounters the living God in this sacramental union. It unites their lives with Christ's saving actions. In this sacrament, God continues to save his people.

All this is much more important than the common "wedding planning guide" can begin to comprehend. "How many bridesmaids and groomsmen can participate?" is a *moment question* that requires a simple answer. "How does this celebration of marriage affect a change of heart in this couple? How can it effect a deeper conversion to God through the Church? How will this couple participate in the mission of Christ for the life of the world?" These are *forever questions*. The consequences of these answers are broad and deep.

ALWAYS BEGIN WITH THE RITE

When preparing any liturgy of the Church, always begin with the rite. From the Introduction (*praenotanda*) of *The Order of Celebrating Matrimony*, one can glean the theology of the sacrament, the intent of the rite, and the practicalities of its proper celebration. The texts of *The Order of Celebrating Matrimony* express the beliefs of the Church. Therefore, the texts should be respected and unaltered.

It is important to use the most recent edition of any ritual book. Thus, the second typical edition of *The Order of Celebrating Matrimony* (2016) is the most current edition of the rite. In the United States this edition may be used on September 8, 2016 (the Feast of the Nativity of the Blessed Virgin Mary). Its use is mandatory on and after December 30, 2016 (the Feast of the Holy Family of Jesus, Mary, and Joseph).

THE WORD OF GOD IS INTEGRAL TO THE RITE

Sacred Scripture is integral to any Catholic liturgy and *The Order of Celebrating Matrimony* is no exception. The revealed Word of God lays a firm foundation for the sacrament and places this liturgy, this bride and groom, in the context of Salvation History

Given that the purposes of worship are to praise God and to make humans more holy, the *Introduction of the Lectionary for Mass* says:

> [The] participation of the faithful in the Liturgy increases to the degree that, as they listen to the Word of God proclaimed in the Liturgy, they strive harder to commit themselves to the Word of God incarnate in Christ. Thus, they endeavor to conform their way of life to what they celebrate in the Liturgy, and then in turn to bring to the celebration of the Liturgy all that they do in life (LMI 6).

The presider is reminded numerous times in the Introduction to the *Lectionary for Mass* to select Scriptural options "for the good of the faithful." The readings which the Church has selected for *The Order of Celebrating Matrimony* have a bounty of advice on living as husband and wife. The Scripture readings become the source for the Homily and directly affects the selection of music texts used within the wedding liturgy.

LITURGY IS MUSICAL

The Church expects certain parts of the liturgy to be sung, especially those parts when the presider engages the assembly in dialogue. For instance, the dialogues of the Introductory Rite, the Gospel Acclamation, and the acclamations during the Eucharistic Prayer, are to be sung. Some elements are sung by their very nature — the Responsorial Psalm and the Gloria are sung because they are hymns of praise. In addition, the liturgical assembly may sing hymns and other chants to accompany a liturgical action.

Music has the ability to express a wide dimension of meaning, feelings, and intuitions that words alone cannot. Music, particularly singing, is a primary means of participation. It is not meant to fill times of silence. There are places where instrumental music is appropriate and elsewhere not.

The music chosen for a wedding liturgy must, first and foremost, serve the liturgy and express the faith. Many couples will want to include "their favorite song," but these are most likely more appropriate for the reception and not the wedding liturgy.

> Secular music, even though it may emphasize the love of the spouses for one another, is not appropriate for the Sacred Liturgy. Songs that are chosen for the liturgy should be appropriate for the celebration and express the faith of the Church (SL 220).

Elsewhere in this Pastoral Companion you will find more detailed information about choosing music for a Catholic wedding liturgy.

OPTIONS ARE NOT OPTIONAL

Church ministers and engaged couples are *preparing* what the Church has already *planned*. Thus, the rite is not invented anew. Instead, one makes careful selections from among the many options provided. And *The Order of Celebrating Matrimony* is rich with options designed to accommodate various pastoral circumstances! When options are provided in any liturgical text, one must choose from among those options. "Option" assumes one is making a choice. Option does not mean "making this part up" or dismissing the required choices. Any occasion for invention or adaptation will be clearly marked by phrases such as "in these or similar words."

LITURGY SHOULD LOOK LIKE LITURGY.

Next, a Catholic wedding should look like Catholic liturgy. This is, above all, worship of almighty God. This celebration should be as reverent, as well prepared, and as dignified as every act of worship. It should invite prayerful participation and display the dynamics and essential qualities of Catholic worship. While choices need to be made in a number of areas, the wedding liturgy has a structure that is familiar to many Catholics.

THE COUPLE SHOULD BE INVOLVED IN THE LITURGY'S PREPARATION

"The celebration itself of the Sacrament must be diligently prepared, as far as possible, with the engaged couple" (OCM 29). With appropriate catechesis and resources, the engaged couple can become well formed in the rite itself and should be invited to participate in preparing the liturgy. With guidance from the Priest or Deacon, they can intelligently choose from among the options — selecting readings, prayers, and processions that are both meaningful to them and to the faith of the Church. Then, and only then, can they more deeply and freely enter into the ritual which expresses their love for each other, God's love for them, and the mystery of God's salvific love for the world.

THE ENTIRE ASSEMBLY CELEBRATES THE LITURGY

The Constitution on the Sacred Liturgy reminds us that ... "every liturgical celebration is an action of Christ the priest and of his Body the Church ..." (SC 7). Thus, every person present has an important role in the celebration. Every person present is invited to celebrate the Paschal Mystery of Jesus Christ. They, too, are nourished by the Word of God and enriched by the rite. They, too, are invited to give God praise.

Friends and family should not act as mere observers, but should be enabled to participate fully, consciously, and actively. It is both their privilege and responsibility to witness the Consent. They are called together to support the bride and groom, not only on the wedding day, but for years to come. To do that, they need to enter into the prayer and power of the liturgy.

Often, the Introductions of liturgical books will remind the presider to choose texts "for the good of the faithful." This is a good reminder that what we choose and how we prepare affects people's faith. A related question might be "How will this choice affect the assembly's participation?" Even practical choices, such as the placement of the couple, the arrangement of the seating, and the volume of the microphone will affect the participation of the people.

It is the duty of the parish ministers to facilitate participation by providing worship aids and, occasionally, gentle instruction. A worship aid should include all the people's parts, sung or recited. Page 101 of this book offers a guide for preparing just such an aid. (*The Gift of Love: A Bride and Grooms' Guide to Preparing the Wedding Liturgy* is also available from FDLC. In very conversational language, it offers the couple liturgical catechesis, helpful guides and useful tools. Chapter Five addresses the worship aid.)

LITURGICAL MINISTERS SERVE THE LITURGICAL ASSEMBLY

Some members of the assembly will have roles as liturgical ministers. Whether they are parish ministers or those selected from among family and friends, those with liturgical roles should be qualified, competent, and carefully rehearsed.

DIOCESAN AND PARISH GUIDELINES ARE IMPORTANT

It is assumed that diocesan and parish guidelines have been established regarding Marriage preparation, liturgical celebrations, sacramental issues, and canonical requirements. Policies regarding dispensations, delegations, and liturgical law are to be respected (cf. Canon 1066 and OCM nos. 19, 24, 27).

EVERY ENCOUNTER IS AN OPPORTUNITY FOR COMPASSIONATE, PASTORAL MINISTRY

In all areas of marriage preparation, couples and their families should expect patience and kindness from the Priest or Deacon, the parish staff members, and the parish musicians whom they encounter. Is it the Priest or Deacon's role to make everyone happy? Obviously not. Sometimes, the couple's requests will not or cannot be granted. Priests or Deacons might begin with the fact that many couples simply have little knowledge of Catholic liturgy. Patient catechesis, tact, and compassion may be required.

CHAPTER FOUR:
Preparing the Marriage Liturgy

The Order of Celebrating Matrimony encourages presiders to prepare the wedding liturgy with the engaged couple. With the advice of the presider, together they may choose:

- the liturgical day and season
- the rite (OCM: Chapter I, II or III)
- the liturgical ministers
- the form of the entrance procession
- the Scripture readings
- the Mass propers as found in the *Roman Missal* [for Rite I]
- the texts from *The Order of Celebrating Matrimony*
  - the formula and method for the Consent
  - the formularies for the Blessing and Giving of Rings
  - the inclusion of cultural adaptations
  - the text of the Nuptial Blessing
- the composition of the Universal Prayers
- cultural adaptations
- liturgical music — including hymns, psalms, dialogues and acclamations
- the arrangement of the environment
- posture, placement, and movement during the liturgy

Preparing what the Church has planned requires a collaborative effort. Priests or Deacons want to guide a couple to a better understanding of what is being celebrated — God's love for this couple through the Liturgy of the Church — while providing opportunities for the couple to best express their unique love and pastoral circumstances.

BEST PRACTICES

Are there such things as "best practices"? The liturgical answer to this question is "yes." Some decisions should be based upon those practices which have been proven to work effectively and reverently. These practices have consistently supported the liturgical prayer of the Church. These practices have effectively supported the ministerial roles within the liturgy. These practices have supported the full, conscious and active participation of the assembly. Most importantly, these practices have strengthened, not weakened, the faith being expressed.

So, these pages will offer recommendations for "best practices." We offer them not because they are traditional, easier, or popular, but because they enact the rite and engage the assembly. A best practice helps make a marriage liturgy more prayerful, participatory, and powerful.

THE CHOICE OF DAY

There are certain days during the liturgical year when the Ritual Mass "For the *Celebration of Marriage*" may not be used. These days are holy to the worldwide Church. The Church observes them with greater solemnity. Other rites, including *The Order of Celebrating Matrimony*, are secondary to what we are universally observing that day. The Mass of the Day is celebrated, with the addition of the Nuptial Blessing and, if appropriate, the proper formula for the final blessing.

These solemn days are ranked as "1 through 4" in the "Table of Liturgical Days According to their Order of Precedence" (Universal Norms for the Liturgical Year and the Calendar, 59). They are:

1. Easter Triduum of the Lord's Passion and Resurrection

2. Christmas, Epiphany, Ascension, and Pentecost
    Sundays of Advent, Lent, and the Easter Season
    Ash Wednesday
    Weekdays of Holy Week (Monday to Thursday, inclusive)
    Days within the Octave of Easter

3. Solemnities of the Lord, the Blessed Virgin Mary, and saints listed in the
    General Calendar
    The Commemoration of All the Faithful Departed (All Souls)

4. The solemnity of the principal patron of the place
    The solemnity of the dedication of the parish church
    The solemnity of the Title of a particular church (e.g., Sacred Heart)
    The solemnity of the title, founder, or patron of a religious order

Every Sunday, too, is important. In a particular way, "the Church celebrates the paschal mystery on the first day of the week, known as the Lord's Day or Sunday. This follows a tradition handed down from the Apostles and having its origin from the day of Christ's resurrection. Thus Sunday must be ranked as the first holy day of all" (SC 106, UNLYC 4). In some dioceses, a wedding may take place at a Sunday Mass in Ordinary Time. Celebrating a wedding within a regular parish Sunday liturgy holds in tension both the liturgical requirements needed for a parish Mass (prayers, Scripture, music) and a couple's options within the OCM. The Mass texts of the Sunday are used. However, one of the Scripture readings which explicitly speaks of Marriage may be taken from *The Order of Celebrating Matrimony* (OCM 144-187; cf. *Lectionary for Mass, Volume IV*, nos. 801-805).

If a wedding liturgy is scheduled on a Sunday (or perhaps late Saturday evening) and it is not a Mass in which the entire parish community participates, one may choose the ritual Mass texts (OCM 34b). This Mass, too, fulfills the Sunday obligation of those Catholics who attend.

In summary, the following list might provide a simple, chronological list of those days on which the Ritual Mass is not used:

First Sunday of Advent
Second Sunday of Advent
Immaculate Conception of the BVM (December 8)
Third Sunday of Advent
Fourth Sunday of Advent
Nativity of the Lord/ Christmas (December 25)
Mary, the Holy Mother of God (January 1)
Epiphany of the Lord
Ash Wednesday
First Sunday of Lent
Second Sunday of Lent
Third Sunday of Lent
Fourth Sunday of Lent
Fifth Sunday of Lent
Saint Joseph, Spouse of the BVM (March 19)
Annunciation of the Lord (March 25)
Palm Sunday of the Passion of the Lord
Monday of Holy Week
Tuesday of Holy Week
Wednesday of Holy Week
Thursday of Holy Week (day)
Holy Thursday
Good Friday
Holy Saturday/ Easter Vigil
Easter Sunday

Monday within the Octave of Easter
Tuesday within the Octave of Easter
Wednesday within the Octave of Easter
Thursday within the Octave of Easter
Friday within the Octave of Easter
Saturday within the Octave of Easter
Second Sunday of Easter/ Sunday of Divine Mercy
Third Sunday of Easter
Fourth Sunday of Easter
Fifth Sunday of Easter
Sixth Sunday of Easter
Ascension of the Lord
Seventh Sunday of Easter
Pentecost
The Most Holy Trinity
The Most Holy Body and Blood of Christ
The Most Sacred Heart of Jesus
Nativity of John the Baptist (June 24)
Saints Peter and Paul (June 29)
Assumption of the Blessed Virgin Mary (August 15)
All Saints (November 1)
Commemoration of all the Faithful Departed (November 2)
Our Lord Jesus Christ, King of the Universe

This order will be impacted by the date of Easter in any given year.

The liturgical season also governs the celebration:

> If a Marriage is celebrated on a day having a penitential character, especially during Lent, the pastor is to counsel the spouses to take into account the special nature of that day (OCM 32).

However, when the Ritual Mass *"For the Celebration of Marriage"* is selected, some liturgical elements will be impacted. For instance, if a wedding between two Catholics on a weekday in Advent, the *Glory to God* would be sung or said and the color of vestments would be white, not violet. The Advent wreath and the seasonal environment would remain in place.

THE CHOICE OF PLACE

Just as we design and shape the spaces we occupy, spaces form us. We feel and behave differently in a formal mansion or an historic monument than we do in a summer cabin or a seashore retreat. Liturgical space is no different.

While God is certainly everywhere, a church is God's house and the place where the people of God worship him. The Catholic Church considers a church to be the proper environment for the celebration of the sacraments.

To secular society, this practice might seem difficult to comprehend. Some may think that "one space is as good as another." Yet, if that assumption is true, we ignore the power of what the spaces we occupy represent. For instance, a professional baseball game is not played on a hockey rink; the President of a nation is not inaugurated in a stadium.

A sacrament is a holy thing and it deserves a holy place. The wedding liturgy is not just a venue for observing an engaged couple's change in legal status. This intimately involves God and our best selves. The Church is encountering the living God and making present, through the Holy Spirit, his divine grace at work in the lives of this particular couple. The Church community acknowledges and participates in this sacred action. A beach, a mountaintop, or a public space that is used for varied functions cannot bear the weight of this Mystery.

In addition, *The Order of Celebrating Matrimony* presumes that all present will fully, consciously and actively participate in the liturgy of the Church. This expectation is not given naively. In order to fully, consciously and actively participate in the liturgy, there are expected standards of quality from the ministers: being able to see, to hear, to acclaim, to sing and to celebrate the ritual. One must be able to pay attention to what is being said/sung. One deserves the ability to focus on what is happening within oneself, around oneself, and in relationship to others. All this is required for celebrating the liturgy.

"The Marriage is to be celebrated in the parish of one or other of the engaged persons, or elsewhere with the permission of the proper Ordinary or pastor" (OCM 27). Here, by "elsewhere" the rite means other Catholic chapels or churches.

"A marriage between Catholics or between a Catholic party and a non-Catholic baptized party is to be celebrated in a parish church. It can be celebrated in another church or oratory with the permission of the local Ordinary or pastor (Canon 1118.1). The permission of the local Bishop is required for the wedding liturgy to take place in a suitable place outside of a Catholic church (Canon 1118.2). Please check with your chancery for policies and necessary dispensations.

Some may complain that using the church building is somehow more expensive than not. There may well be a cost for the use of some parish church buildings. A wedding can be very simple or very elaborate and costs for many details will differ. If a couple really has financial difficulties, then a conversation with the pastor can explore the possibility of waiving any fees. Money should not be the starting point nor ending point of whether or not to marry in the Catholic Church.

So, is it impossible to have a Catholic wedding outside of a Catholic Church building? Not impossible. A Bishop can grant a dispensation for a good cause, but this will be rare.

RESPECTING CULTURE'S PROFOUND INFLUENCE

We cannot escape that all of us live within a culture. The word "culture" describes many things — repeated practices, historic traditions, prevailing attitudes, and long-held beliefs. Sometimes it is called upon to rationalize what we prefer to do or not to do.

Culture, too, has a profound influence on our prayer. Over many centuries, our liturgies have been influenced by rites and rituals, languages and laws, people and practices, ancient texts and modern thought. Even in our own times, Catholic identity can be strengthened when we appreciate and respect how various cultures worship. Even in diversity, we can find common ground.

There has been and continues to be a demographic shift in many Catholic communities across the United States. Some urban areas have seen a decline in population while others have increased. Some ethnicities have seen a growth in population while others have seen a decline. Some parishes are made up of multiple cultural groups and may celebrate liturgies in more than one language.

What does this mean for a Catholic wedding? It means that the Priest or Deacon who is preparing the liturgy will need to be attuned to the cultural heritages of the bride and groom. Language, traditions, music, and other non-verbal elements may need to be considered.

In the helpful guide, *Liturgy in a Culturally Diverse Community* (FDLC, 2012) these and other issues are considered. This guide describes an "*Intercultural Spirituality*" based on mutual respect and charity:

> If spirituality can be defined as a way one understands and acts on the movements of God's spirit on human life, then helping people attend to how God in Christ is manifesting the divine presence in a multicultural context could be a description of an intercultural spirituality. Modeling an attitude of listening, patience and at times sacrifice will be an important role ... As the document Music in Catholic Worship wisely pointed out "Each Christian must keep in mind that to live and worship in community often demands a personal sacrifice. All must be willing to share likes and dislikes with others whose ideas and experiences may be quite unlike their own" (LCDC 9).

Within the revised *Order of Celebrating Matrimony,* approved cultural adaptations are given as options. These are bracketed within the ritual text for convenience. These may not be relevant to every bride and groom.

PART III

Examining the Elements of the Rites

As in the 1969 rite, the second edition provides three distinct rites, each suited to the particular circumstances of each couple. Pastoral circumstances may refer to the faith life of the couple, their baptismal status, or the realities of extended families. These do not refer to previous marriage issues or conditions. An engaged couple can expect that the priest or deacon working with them will give them insight on which is the most appropriate option for them.

Chapter I: *The Order of Celebrating Matrimony within Mass* (OCM 45-78)

When two Catholics marry, the celebration normally takes place within Mass (OCM 29). The Mass texts are taken from the "Ritual Mass V: For the Celebration of Marriage" if the liturgical day permits or from the Mass of the Day when the liturgical day does not permit the use of the Ritual Mass. The presider for *Celebrating the Order of Marriage Within Mass* is a priest. A deacon may assist the priest, but the priest who presides should preach, receive the consent and offer the *Nuptial Blessing* (OCM 23).

Many pastoral situations are presented when a couple seeks marriage. There are occasions when a Catholic couple may ask for the *Order of Celebrating Matrimony without Mass* because it appears to take less time that the Order within Mass. There may be times when so many of those who are gathered for the wedding would not be Catholic (for example when either the bride or groom was recently welcomed into the Church). But the Catholic bride and groom have a right to a wedding Mass. These kinds of requests require patient listening and careful evangelizing to encourage the value of the Eucharist in the spiritual life of the engaged couple.

> Although pastors are ministers of Christ's Gospel for all, they should, nonetheless, direct special attention to those, whether Catholics or non-Catholics, who never or rarely take part in the celebration of Marriage or the Eucharist. This pastoral norm applies in the first place to the spouses themselves (OCM 37).

Chapter II: *The Order of Celebrating Matrimony without Mass* (OCM 79-117)

When a Catholic marries another baptized Christian, the celebration normally takes place outside of Mass. The presider would be either a priest or a deacon. This rite includes the Introductory Rites, the Liturgy of the Word, the Celebration of Matrimony including the Nuptial Blessing, and the Conclusion of the Celebration. There is an option for the Distribution of Holy Communion for Catholic participants

Sometimes, a couple may ask to celebrate Mass even though one of them is not Catholic. This would require the permission of the local Bishop. To discern this kind of pastoral challenge presumes good will by all and can be an opening, not only for the engaged couple, but their families as well to experience the hospitality of the Church who prays. If the situation warrants it, *The Order for Celebrating Matrimony Within Mass* (OCM 45-78) may be used, with the consent of the local Ordinary; but with regard to the admission of a non-Catholic party to Eucharistic Communion, the norms issued for various cases are to be observed (CIC 844, OCM 36).

One should question if this choice is ideal, since the celebration of Mass might be very unfamiliar to many in attendance. Perhaps the community might focus on what all can share, i.e., the Word of God and the beauty of the celebration of Marriage.

Chapter III: *The Order of Celebrating Matrimony Between a Catholic and a Catechumen or a Non-Christian* (OCM 118-143)

When a Catholic marries a non-baptized person this rite "is to be used" (OCM 36). No other option is given nor permitted. The structure is simple — The Rite of Reception, the Liturgy of the Word, the Celebration of Matrimony, and the Conclusion of the Celebration.

Now, let us look at each of the three rites in detail.

CHAPTER FIVE:
About *The Order of Celebrating Matrimony Within Mass*

The Introductory Rites

- Greeting of the Bride and Groom
  (or after the procession)
- Entrance Procession
- Entrance Song
- Sign of the Cross
- Greeting of the People
- Introduction
- Glory to God
- Collect

The Liturgy of the Word

- First Reading
- Responsorial Psalm
- Second Reading
- Gospel Acclamation
- Gospel
- Homily

The Celebration of Matrimony

- Address to the Bride and Groom
- The Questions before the Consent
- The Consent
- The Reception of the Consent
- The Blessing and Giving of Rings
- [The Blessing and Giving of the *Arras*]
- [Hymn or Canticle of Praise]
- The Universal Prayer (Prayer of the Faithful)

The Liturgy of the Eucharist

- Presentation of the Gifts
- Prayer over the Offerings
- Eucharistic Prayer
- [The Blessing and Placing of the *Lazo* or the Veil]
- The Lord's Prayer
- Nuptial Blessing
- Sign of Peace
- Distribution of Holy Communion
- Period of Silent Prayer
- Prayer after Communion

The Conclusion of the Celebration

- Solemn Blessing
- The Recessional

THE INTRODUCTORY RITES

A LITTLE HISTORY

This English translation of the *Order of Celebrating Matrimony* is used in English-speaking Conferences throughout the world. The draft which the U.S. Bishops approved in November 2013 included instructions for a greeting and a procession very similar to the 1969 ritual edition for the dioceses of the United States, which read:

> At the appointed time, the priest, vested for Mass, goes with the ministers to the door of the church or, if more suitable, to the altar. There he greets the bride and bridegroom in a friendly manner, showing that the Church shares their joy ... If there is to be a procession to the altar, the ministers go first, followed by the priest, and then the bride and bridegroom. According to local custom, they may be escorted by at least their parents and the two witnesses. Meanwhile, the entrance song is sung (RM 1969, nos. 19-20).

> The procession to the altar then takes place: The servers go first, the minister(s) follows, and then the couple who, according to local custom, may be accompanied as a sign of honor by at least their parents and the two witnesses, to the place prepared for them. Meanwhile, the Entrance Chant takes place (OCM 46, 2013 draft edition).

In the end, the 2016 edition of the rite still contained two forms for the Greeting of the Couple and two options for the Entrance Procession. However, the Congregation for Divine Worship and the Discipline of the Sacraments observed that English-speaking countries all had worthy practices for the Entrance Procession. So, a small adjustment was made in order to respect this variety of cultural practices. The rubric now reads:

> "The procession to the altar then takes place in the customary manner. Meanwhile the Entrance Chant takes place" (OCM 46, 2016 edition).

THE GREETING OF THE BRIDE AND GROOM

The Priest, in the name of the Church, greets the bridal party. There is no prescribed text for this greeting but the instruction says that the Priest "greets the bridal party warmly, showing that the Church shares in their joy" (OCM 45).

This may take two forms. The first form assumes that the Priest is part of the entrance procession. The second assumes that he waits in the sanctuary.

Form One: Greeting of the bridal party at the doors of the church before the Entrance procession (45-47).

Form Two: The Priest goes with the servers to the place prepared for the couple or to his chair. When they arrive at their place, he greets the bride and groom. During the entrance chant, the Priest approaches the altar, reverences it with a profound bow, and venerates it with a kiss. After this, he goes to his chair (48-50).

The First Form and the Second Form are about "greeting" the couple by the minister. Looking at these forms more closely we discover that the primary difference between the First Form and the Second Form is when and where the greeting is given by the priest to the bride and groom. Meeting them at the door implies that the bride and groom are standing together. (In some cultures this presents a problem, as the engaged couple are not supposed to "see each other" until the bride walks down the aisle. This prohibition is a superstition; however, to some, it may be a strong omen.)

Having the Priest greet someone at the doors of the church is not that unusual among the rituals of the Church. It is mentioned in *The Rite of Baptism for Children*, *The Order of Christian Funerals*, and the *Rite of Acceptance into the Order of Catechumens*. It is unusual that in *The Order of Celebrating Matrimony*, such a greeting is to be done privately. In the earlier edition of the rite, the greeting could be omitted, with the celebration of marriage beginning "at once with Mass" (RM 19).

In the Second Form, the Priest and servers go to the place where he is to greet the couple. One might assume that the Priest and servers are moving from the sacristy or vesting room to the sanctuary; no specifics are given about how this entrance is to be done — whether the Priest or Deacon enters down the center aisle or if he enters from the sanctuary — or where these "places" are located. In other words, the rubrics are generously vague (OCM 48-49). It assumes they are not part of the procession of the bridal party. It does assume that there is an entrance chant and that during it, the priest reverences the altar with a profound bow, venerates it with a kiss, and goes to his chair (OCM 50).

THE ENTRANCE PROCESSION

As in most of our liturgical celebrations, an entrance procession begins an act of worship. A procession not only moves people from one place to another. It is, in itself, an act of gathering — ministers usually process down an aisle through the midst of the assembly.

The 1969 edition of the rite gave two forms for the greeting of the couple, but only provided details on the entrance procession with the ministers (see RM no. 20, above).

While both the First Form and Second Form remain in the revised 2016 text, few details are provided for the procession. Because this English translation serves a variety of countries and cultures, *The Order of Celebrating Matrimony* simply states, "The procession to the altar then takes place in the customary manner. Meanwhile the Entrance Chant takes place" (OCM 46). The rubric gives no instruction beyond "in the customary manner" (ibid). It allows for broad interpretation.

Still, it might be valuable to examine best practices regarding an entrance procession.

BEST PRACTICE

If you have attended a Catholic wedding, the beginning of the wedding usually does not look the same as the beginning of Sunday Mass. Perhaps the reason for this is that different cultures and eras have developed ways to highlight the entrance of the bride and/or the groom. In some traditions, the father of the bride was seen to "give away" the daughter to her husband as part of a marriage contract, an exchange of property for a dowry. The bride's place in an entrance procession became highlighted and the practice became commonplace. Few modern couples know the historic precedents of "giving the bride away."

Keeping the sense of a liturgical procession is a great value. Liturgy should begin with a liturgical procession. Ideally, the procession should be led by a processional cross. It should include the liturgical ministers. It might also include the bridesmaids and groomsmen as well as the maid/matron of honor and the best man.

The parents of both the bride and groom should participate. The bride and groom each were formed by their parents (or step parents). Both mother and father were instrumental in their creation and upbringing. There are certainly complications which can arise with such a best practice: such as having a deceased parent or parents who are divorced. That's the messiness of life. However, by encouraging parents to be a part of the entrance procession acknowledges a past and a future, a coming and a going, and a welcoming into a new extended family. This will have meaning for moms and dads, groom and bride, and all who witness it.

Since weddings happen with all kinds of expectations, sometimes the composition of the entrance procession seeks to showcase the closest friends of the bride and groom; or to highlight some unique aspect of the bride and groom. While meaningful to the couple, some requests can overwhelm the liturgical procession. Sometimes, it appears inappropriate to feature children or to have an extremely large number of people in the wedding party. Is this in harmony with the liturgy of the Church? Weddings are often considered public, social events; other, secular images of weddings influence choices. However, gentle guidance by the presider or parish staff can shape an Entrance Procession which follows liturgical norms.

A liturgical procession does not assume that the bride enters alone nor that the focus of the procession is on just the bride. The liturgical procession allows the liturgical ministers to enter the Church, and helps the liturgical assembly to enter into what is to come. Here is a sample for an Order of Procession:

- Cross bearer
- Servers
- Readers
- [Assisting Deacon]
- Bridesmaids and Groomsmen
- Maid/Matron of Honor and Best Man
- Bride and Groom (three options for entry)
    Bride and Groom together
    Groom with parents; Bride with parents
    Groom; then Bride

There should be no change of music for the bride — the bride and groom are equal partners in this covenant relationship. Instead, the music which accompanies the procession might be an instrumental version of the Entrance Chant [Opening Hymn]. When all have reached their places, a well-trained pastoral musician can lead the assembly directly into the verses of the Opening Hymn.

While the 1969 Rite allowed for the "rite of welcome to be omitted" (RM 19), the revised Rite does not speak of that provision within Mass. [It does give the option to omit the Rite of Reception in Rite III: *The Order of Celebrating Matrimony between a Catholic and a Catechumen or Non-Christian* (OCM 121].

THE SIGN OF THE CROSS AND GREETING

The priest makes the Sign of the Cross, then greets the assembly using one of the greeting options given in The Roman Missal.

THE INTRODUCTORY ADDRESS

Then the priest offers an introduction to the celebration. Two options are provided in edition (OCM 52-53). The first is addressed to the assembly, the second is addressed to the couple. Of course, either of these texts may be replaced with "similar words" prepared by the presider.

THE PENITENTIAL ACT

The rubrics in this edition clearly state that "The Penitential Act is omitted." This is in harmony with other Masses which begin with a welcoming rite, such as at a funeral, the baptism of a child within Mass, or the Rite of Acceptance into the Order of Catechumens (cf. GIRM 46).

THE GLORY TO GOD

When the Sacrament of Matrimony is celebrated within the Ritual Mass, the Glory to God is always sung or said. This directive appears *The Roman Missal, third edition* (GIRM 53 and in the rubrics for the Ritual Masses). Even on a weekday of Advent and Lent, the Gloria is sung or said.

If the sacrament of Matrimony is celebrated on a day on which the Ritual Mass may not be used, the Gloria is sung/said only if prescribed for that day. For example, on the Solemnity of the Assumption, the Gloria is prescribed for the day. On a Sunday of Advent or Lent, the Gloria would not be sung or said, but neither would the texts for the ritual Mass be used on those Sundays.

COLLECT

The 1969 edition had four options for the Collect (Opening Prayer). This edition has six new or newly-translated Collects (OCM 188-193). These are already found in *The Roman Missal, third edition.* The OCM does provide one caveat — the Collect found at no. 188 should not be chosen when one uses the first option for the Nuptial Blessing (OCM 74). The texts of both prayers are too similar and the texts would be redundant.

When the Ritual Mass is not celebrated, the Collect is taken from the Mass of the Day.

BEST PRACTICE — The Placement of Couple and Witnesses

The purpose of the Introductory Rites "is to ensure that the faithful, who come together as one, establish communion and dispose themselves properly to listen to the Word of God and to celebrate the Eucharist worthily" (GIRM 46).

Where should the couple and witnesses be positioned by the conclusion of the Introductory Rites? Certainly this will vary depending on the size and arrangement of the sanctuary and the nave of each church.

During the Mass, the couple needs to take the same postures as all the members of the assembly. They need to be able to sit, stand and kneel. It is best to have the couple be physically positioned to focus their attention in these ways. Variations can be made so that the ministers of the liturgy and the couple (the ministers of the sacrament) can be seen as collaboratively engaged in prayer.

In many cases, there are more than two witnesses in the bridal party. Where they are to stand at the conclusion of the procession would also be determined by the size and the configuration of the worship space. Typically, they are seated in the nave of the church, near the sanctuary.

THE READINGS

The revised rite notes that "the Liturgy of the Word is celebrated in the usual manner" (OCM 55). There may be three Scripture readings. The First Reading is from the Old Testament, except during the fifty days of the Easter Season when it is taken from Revelation (OCM 55).

The Scriptural texts for the Celebration of Marriage are printed in their entirety in Chapter Four of the OCM: "Various Texts to be Use in the Rite of Marriage and in the Mass for the Celebration of Marriage" (OCM 144-187). These same readings may be found in *The Lectionary for Mass, Volume IV*, nos. 801-805.

There is a new stipulation that at least one reading, which speaks explicitly speaks of Marriage must always be chosen (OCM 55). Within Chapter Four, the readings that explicitly speak of Marriage have an asterisk beside the citation.

When, according to the "Table of Liturgical Days According to Their Order of Precedence" (*Universal Norms on the Liturgical Year and the Calendar*, no. 59), the Ritual Mass may not be celebrated, the readings are taken from The Lectionary for Mass as prescribed for that day. But one reading, which explicitly speaks of Marriage, may be substituted.

For a complete list of the readings, please see pages 56-58 herein.

OLD TESTAMENT AND NEW TESTAMENT READINGS

In order to be compatible with *The Lectionary for Mass* (1997-1999), this new edition of the OCM includes some additional readings. Proverbs 31:10-13, 19-20, 30-31 has been added to the list of Old Testament readings. This reading explicitly refers to marriage. It is marked with an asterisk. The reading from Sirach will be cited at "Sirach 26:1-4, 13-16" in *The Lectionary for Mass* — the verses used in the New American Bible translation. In the Vulgate translation, the citation will read "Sirach 26:1-4, 16-21." The content is the same; the verse numbering is distinct. So, if you see "Vg." before the citation, it's simply taken from the Vulgate edition. Both are listed in the ritual edition.

Four *pericopes* have been added to the options for the New Testament reading — Romans 15:1b-3a, 5-7, 13; Philippians 4:4-9; Hebrews 13:1-4a, 5-6b, and Ephesians 4:1-6. All but Ephesians are found in the *Lectionary* at no. 802. This apparently was an oversight when the *Lectionary* was prepared. But one can easily find the Ephesian reading just a few pages away at no. 807 (among the options for the Ritual Mass for the Blessing of Abbots and Abbesses). The OCM also provides the complete texts of the seven options for the Responsorial Psalm. These seven selections are the same as in the 1969 edition, but the translation in the OCM is drawn from the *Revised Grail Psalter*. The translation of these seven psalms in the *Lectionary for Mass* is taken from the NAB. Either translation is permissible until a new *Lectionary* is promulgated.

THE RESPONSORIAL PSALM

A psalm follows the First Reading. Since a psalm is a song, the text is normally sung. The music minister may suggest various settings for the Responsorial Psalm. The psalm is from Scripture and may not be replaced by a song (GIRM 61.3).

> The chants to be sung during the Rite of Marriage should be appropriate and should express the faith of the Church, with attention paid to the importance of the Responsorial Psalm within the Liturgy of the Word. What is said concerning the chants applies also to the selection of other musical works (OCM 30).

ALLELUIA VERSE OR VERSE BEFORE THE GOSPEL

The Alleluia Verse or Verse before the Gospel is typically sung. During Lent, the Alleluia is omitted and the Gospel Acclamation begins with "Praise to you, Lord Jesus Christ, King of endless glory," "Glory to you, O word of God, Lord Jesus Christ," "Praise and honor to you, Lord Jesus Christ," or "Glory and praise to you, Lord Jesus Christ." The OCM also suggests an acclamation which may be new to the dioceses of the United States. It lists "Sing joyfully to God our strength" (Psalm 81:2). The music minister may suggest various settings for the acclamation.

The four verses are the same ones which were prescribed in 1969, but they have been newly-translated. All four are taken from the First Letter of John, chapter four. They may be found in *The Lectionary for Mass* at no. 804.

THE GOSPEL

The Gospel *pericopes* for the celebration of Marriage are the same as in the 1969 edition. They are taken from the Gospel according to Matthew, Mark, and John. They may be found in *The Lectionary for Mass*, no. 805 and in Chapter Four of the OCM, nos. 178-187.

THE HOMILY

The Homily should be based on the Scripture readings. In addition to the sacred texts, the *Introduction to the Order of Celebrating Matrimony* (OCM 1-11) provides a valuable resource in preparing the Homily. These paragraphs contain a wealth of theology on the Sacrament of Matrimony, some of which may be challenging and counter-cultural.

It may be that many people in attendance at the wedding are unchurched or have little familiarity with the Christian Scriptures. The Priest should speak of God's faithful love; tell of how Christ uses the image of a wedding feast to describe both human and divine love; tell of the need for faithful married love in a world that fears commitment and is obsessed with selfishness. The couple (and the entire liturgical assembly) can be reminded of the presence of God within their marriage. All present can be encouraged to nurture their sacramental union through prayer, especially by participation in the Eucharist. Will the homily encourage the newly-married couple into the world to witness to the love of Christ?

The homily should not be a time to offer a chronological review of a couple's relationship with the priest or each other. Yet, it is not possible to give a Homily at a wedding without reference to the couple. This being said, one can focus on the Sacred Scripture (OCM 29), and how the lives of this couple are related to the readings which have been chosen for this wedding.

> After the reading of the Gospel, the Priest in the Homily uses the sacred text to expound the mystery of Christian Marriage, the dignity of the conjugal love, the grace of the Sacrament, and the responsibilities of married people, keeping in mind, however, the various circumstances of individuals (OCM 57).

BEST PRACTICES

- Always use the *Lectionary* at the wedding liturgy. Scripture should not be proclaimed from a sheet of paper or from a marriage program booklet.
- Non-Biblical readings may not be used during a liturgy.
- It would be helpful to give the couple a full list of the Scripture options. The couple can be asked to consider, "What do you want God to say to you about your married life?" "How do any of these readings interpret your hope for married life?"
- Once the Scripture readings are selected, choosing a musical setting for the psalm and the gospel acclamation will be easier. Hymns should also complement the readings.
- All are expected to be hearers of the Word, thus the placement of the bride and groom should make that possible. One should avoid placing the bride and groom in the sanctuary in such a way that the liturgical assembly focuses on them. Avoid having the couple and witnesses facing away from the Readers and the proclamation of the Word. The entire assembly is seated for the readings before the Gospel, the bride and groom and the entire wedding party should be seated as well.
- Remember, the Word of God is beneficial to those who are about to be married, to those who are already married, and to all the members of the assembly.

READINGS FOR THE CELEBRATION OF MATRIMONY

The Order of Celebrating Matrimony (nos. 144-187) or Lectionary for Mass, Volume IV (nos. 801-805)

Old Testament Reading	Lectionary for Mass 801
• Genesis 1:26-28, 31a*	Male and female he created them.
• Genesis 2:18-24*	The two of them become one body.
• Genesis 24:48-51, 58-67*	In his love for Rebekah, Isaac found solace after the death of his mother.
• Tobit 7:6-14*	May the Lord of heaven prosper you both. May he grant you mercy and peace.
• Tobit 8:4b-8*	Allow us to live together to a happy old age.
• Proverbs 31:10-13, 19-20, 30-31*	The woman who fears the LORD is to be praised.
• Song of Songs 2:8-10, 14, 16a; 8:6-7a	Stern as death is love.
• Sirach 26:1-4, 16-21* (Vg. Sirach 26:1-4, 16-21)	Like the sun rising in the LORD's heaven, the beauty of a virtuous wife is the radiance of her home.
• Jeremiah 31:31-32a, 33-34a	I will make a new covenant with the house of Israel and the house of Judah.

Responsorial Psalm	Lectionary for Mass 803
• Psalm 33:12 and 18, 20-21, 22	The earth is full of the goodness of the Lord.
• Psalm 34:2-3, 4-5, 6-7, 8-9	I will bless the Lord at all times OR Taste and see the goodness of the Lord.
• Psalm 103:1-2, 8 and 13, 17-18a	The Lord is kind and merciful. The Lord's kindness is everlasting to those who fear him.
• Psalm 112:1-2, 3-4, 5-7a, 7bc-8, 9	Blessed the man who greatly delights in the Lord's commands OR Alleluia.
• Psalm 128:1-2, 3, 4-5 *	Blessed are those who fear the Lord OR See how the Lord blesses those who fear him.
• Psalm 145:8-9, 10 and 15, 17-18	How good is the Lord to all (OCM 172).
• Psalm 148:1-2, 3-4, 9-10, 11-13ab, 13c-14a	Let all praise the name of the Lord OR Alleluia.

New Testament Reading	Lectionary for Mass 802
• Romans 8:31b-35, 37-39	What will separate us from the love of Christ?
• Romans 12:1-2, 9-18 (long form) or 1-2, 9-13 (short form)	Offer your bodies as a living sacrifice, holy and pleasing to God.
• Romans 15:1b-3a, 5-7, 13	Welcome one another as Christ welcomed you.
• 1 Corinthians 6:13c-15a, 17-20	Your body is a temple of the Spirit.
• 1 Corinthians 12:31-13:8a	If I do not have love, I gain nothing.
• Ephesians 4:1-6	One Body and one Spirit.
• Ephesians 5:2a, 21-33 * (long form) or 5:2a, 25-32 (short form) *	This a great mystery, but I speak in reference to Christ and the Church.
• Philippians 4:4-9	The God of peace will be with you.
• Colossians 3:12-17	And over all these put on love, that is the bond of perfection.
• Hebrews 13:1-4a, 5-6b *	Let marriage be held in honor by all.
• 1 Peter 3:1-9 *	Be of one mind, sympathetic, loving toward one another.
• 1 John 3:18-24	Love in deed and in truth.
• 1 John 4:7-12	God is love.
• Revelation 19:1, 5-9a	Blessed are those who have been called to the wedding feast of the Lamb.

Alleluia Verse and Verse before the Gospel	Lectionary for Mass 804
• 1 John 4:7b	Everyone who loves is begotten of God and knows God.
• 1 John 4:8b and 11	God is love. Let us love one another, as God has loved us.
• 1 John 4:12	If we love one another, God remains in us and his love is brought to perfection in us.
• 1 John 4:16	Whoever remains in love, remains in God and God in him.

Gospel	Lectionary for Mass 805
• Mathew 5:1-12a	Rejoice and be glad, for your reward will be great in heaven.
• Matthew 5:13-16	You are the light of the world.
• Matthew 7:21, 24-29 (long form) or 7:21, 24-25 (short form)	A wise man built his house on rock.
• Matthew 19:3-6*	What God has united, man must not separate.
• Matthew 22:35-40	This is the greatest and the first commandment. The second is like it.
• Mark 10:6-9*	They are no longer two, but one flesh.
• John 2:1-11*	Jesus did this as the beginning of his signs in Cana in Galilee.
• John 15:9-12	Remain in my love.
• John 15:12-16	This is my commandment: love one another.
• John 17:20-26 (long form) or 17:20-23 (short form)	That they may be brought to perfection as one.

THE CELEBRATION OF MATRIMONY

THE PRESIDER

The presider of *The Order of Celebrating Matrimony within Mass* is to be a Priest. It follows that the presider of this element of the wedding liturgy is the same priest. Even the rubrics enforce this; they refer to the presider as "the Priest."

THE MARRIAGES OF SEVERAL COUPLES

The revised rite indicates that in situations where two or more Marriages are celebrated at the same time, the Questions before the Consent, the Consent itself and the Reception of the Consent must take place individually for each Marriage. The remaining parts, including the Nuptial Blessing, can be spoken once for all using the plural form (OCM 58).

PLACEMENT AND POSTURE

No specifics are given as to where the Priest stands for the Celebration of Matrimony. The design of the church building will dictate logical placements. How can listening be facilitated? Will microphones be required? The Priest may stand with his back to the sanctuary area, while the bride, groom and witnesses have their backs to the assembly. This arrangement can cause difficulties, especially if multiple witnesses create a visual "fence." A way to enhance the assembly's participation could be to have the engaged couple and witnesses stand facing the assembly for the rite itself. In some church buildings this could mean that the couple would stand with their backs to the altar, while the Priest stands in the center aisle or on the apron of the sanctuary.

The OCM indicates that all are standing for the rite, including the couple and witnesses — a posture which indicates attentiveness, interest and participation. "Seeing" is a form of participation. This may be problematic in a small church. Consider how to best include the assembly, visually and aurally, and to physically place the couple in such a way as to permit the assembly to see and hear. The witnesses are positioned near the couple (OCM 59).

THE ADDRESS TO THE COUPLE

The priest addresses the couple in these or similar words:

> Dearly beloved,
> you have come together into the house of the Church,
> so that in the presence of the Church's minister and the community
> your intention to enter into Marriage
> may be strengthened by the Lord with a sacred seal.
> Christ abundantly blesses the love that binds you.
> Through a special Sacrament,
> he enriches and strengthens
> those he has already consecrated by Holy Baptism,
> that they may be faithful to each other for ever
> and assume all the responsibilities of married life.
> And so, in the presence of the Church,
> I ask you to state your intentions.

THE QUESTIONS BEFORE THE CONSENT

This is a new title in the rite. The questions were not identified by a title before this edition.

The 1962 edition of *The Parish Ritual: The Celebration of Marriage*, the question before the consent was the following: "*N., do you take N. here present for your lawful wife/ husband according to the rite of our holy mother, the Church?*" (PR 1-2). This was considered to be the "Consent" of both parties; then the Priest asked the couple to join right hands and to speak in a "clear voice" the "vows," (sic.) repeating after the Priest.

The questions before the consent in the 1969 *Rite of Marriage* were different from the 1962 Parish Ritual. The Priest asked the couple "about their freedom of choice, faithfulness to each other, and the acceptance and upbringing of children" (RM 24).

1969   N. and N., have you come here freely and without reservation   RM 24
        to give yourselves to each other in marriage?

        Will you love and honor each other as man and wife for the rest of your lives?

        Will you accept children lovingly from God,
        and bring them up according to the law of Christ and his Church?

The questions in the 1991 [2016] edition are translated slightly differently:

1991   N. and N., have you come here to enter into Marriage   OCM 69
        without coercion,
        freely and wholeheartedly?

        Are you prepared, as you follow the path of Marriage,
        to love and honor each other
        for as long as you both shall live?

        Are you prepared to accept children lovingly from God
        and to bring them up
        according to the law of Christ and his Church?

As in the 1969 edition, the bride and groom are to answer these questions individually. (The rubric in OCM 60 notes that "each responds separately.") Note the use of the first person singular. They answer: "I have," "I am," and "I am," respectively.

THE CONSENT

The Priest invites the couple to declare their consent and to join their right hands together. The gesture of joining right hands is the same as the 1970 edition of the *Rite of Marriage*. The joining of the right hands evokes the giving of a blood covenant between the two, joining together and forsaking all others. In fact, there is new wording, inviting the couple to enter "*the covenant of Holy Matrimony*" which replaces "*into Marriage.*"

> Priest: Since it is your intention to enter the covenant of Holy Matrimony,
> join your right hands and declare your consent
> before God and his Church.
>
> *They join their right hands.*

Consent — Option One

> Groom: I, N., take you, N., to be my wife.
> I promise to be faithful to you,
> in good times and in bad,
> in sickness and in health,
> to love you and to honor you
> all the days of my life.
>
> Bride: I, N., take you, N., to be my husband.
> I promise to be faithful to you,
> in good times and in bad,
> in sickness and in health,
> to love you and to honor you
> all the days of my life.

Note that the word "*faithful*" replaces the word "*true.*"

Consent — Option Two

This form comes from the Sarum Rite of the 15th century. It was popularized in English- speaking countries and included in the Anglican *Book of Common Prayer*. Since it was in harmony with Catholic theology, the U.S. Bishops included it as an option in the 1969 *Rite of Marriage* and again in the most recent edition.

One line, "to love and to cherish," was not printed in the 1969 edition. It has now been added.

> Groom: I, N., take you, N., for my lawful wife,
> to have and to hold, from this day forward,
> for better, for worse,
> for richer, for poorer,
> in sickness and in health,
> to love and to cherish,
> until death do us part.

Bride: I, N., take you, N., for my lawful husband,
to have and to hold, from this day forward,
for better, for worse,
for richer, for poorer,
in sickness and in health,
to love and to cherish,
until death do us part.

The *Consent* can be given in a number of ways. The couple can repeat each line after the Priest , the couple can memorize the Consent, or the couple can answer "I do" to the words of consent expressed, by the priest, in the interrogatory form (OCM 63).

Priest: N., do you take N., to be your wife? | N., do you take you, N., for your lawful wife,
Do you promise to be faithful to her | to have and to hold, from this day forward,
in good times and in bad, | for better, for worse,
in sickness and in heath, | for richer, for poorer,
to love her and to honor her | in sickness and in health,
all the days of your life? | to love and to cherish
  | until death do you part?

Groom: I do.

Priest: N., do you take N., to be your husband? | N., do you take N., for your lawful husband,
Do you promise to be faithful to him | to have and to hold, from this day forward,
in good times and in bad, | for better, for worse,
in sickness and in heath, | for richer, for poorer,
to love him and to honor him | in sickness and in health,
all the days of your life? | to love and to cherish,
  | until death do you part?

Bride: I do.

To whom does the couple speak during the giving of the Consent? They speak to one another. The Priest merely receives the Consent in the name of the Church. The two official witnesses (and the liturgical assembly) bear witness to this exchange of Consent between the bride and groom.

Often, couples may ask if they can "write their own vows," but no other words of Consent are to be used in a Catholic liturgy.

Canon 1106 allows for the use of an interpreter, if necessary, such as in the case of the request for the Consent in a language not of the presider or in the case of Deaf persons. However, the Canon cautions that the pastor is not to permit it unless he is certain of the trustworthiness of the interpreter.

THE RECEPTION OF THE CONSENT

In the name of the Church, the Priest then receives the couple's Consent. Two options now appear in this edition of *The Order of Celebrating Matrimony* (OCM 64). The word "*asunder*" appears in both options. The phrase also appears in the RSV translation of Matthew 19:6 — "*What therefore God has joined together, let no man put asunder.*"

<u>Option One:</u>

Priest: May the Lord in his kindness strengthen the consent
           you have declared before the Church,
           and graciously bring to fulfillment his blessing within you.
           What God joins together, let no one put asunder.

<u>Option Two: (New)</u>

Priest: May the God of Abraham, the God of Isaac, the God of Jacob,
           the God who joined together our first parents in paradise,
           strengthen and bless in Christ
           the consent you have declared before the Church,
           so that what God joins together, no one may put asunder.

At this point in the rite, it is fitting that the assembly voice some kind of expression of thanks and praise to God for what has just taken place. Thus, the revised rite now includes a new acclamation of praise by the assembly. after the consent.

Priest: Let us bless the Lord.
All: Thanks be to God.

Another acclamation can be sung or said (OCM 65). It can be a sung Alleluia, a psalm response (perhaps the psalm recently used in the Liturgy of the Word), or any psalm of praise. The acclamation is dialogical, between the priest and people. It is an acclamation, not an entire song.

THE BLESSING AND GIVING OF RINGS

The *Blessing and Giving of Rings* follows. The priest may recite the prayer and may sprinkle the rings with holy water. There are three options for the Blessing of the Rings. Only the first option is included within Chapter One (OCM 66), the other two options are found in Chapter Four (OCM 194-195).

Next the bride and groom give each other rings "as the circumstances so suggest." While the 1969 edition had the words "*take this ring,*" the revised rite has "*receive this ring ...*" (OCM 67A). The giving of the rings is a gift to be received from each other. The ring itself is a symbol of uninterrupted, unending love and fidelity. It is usually placed on the third finger of the left hand, which purportedly has a major vein which runs straight to the heart. Both in the 1970 edition and in the revised edition, it is implied that the saying of any words in the giving of rings is optional.

Groom, then Bride:
           N., receive this ring
           as a sign of my love and fidelity.
           In the name of the Father, and of the Son,
           and of the Holy Spirit.

THE BLESSING AND GIVING OF THE *ARRAS*

This rite is an approved cultural adaptation that may be included, especially if this custom is a part of the family's tradition. Yet, no one can be prohibited from using this option.

This practice seems to have its source in the Mozarabic Rite of the fifteenth century. One of the reasons that Bishops of the United States included this option was because of its antiquity. It also appears in the 2010 Spanish edition for the dioceses of the United States — *Ritual del Matrimonio*.

In some cultures, the bride and groom have the tradition of exchanging wedding coins or *arras*. The name comes from "*arrabon*," a Greek word for "pledge." In this rite, the presider blesses the coins, then the bride and groom exchange the coins. This giving of coins is not merely about their own household, but also expresses their charitable concern for others. In some traditions, there are thirteen coins (one for every month and one for charity). Often these ceremonial coins are handed down from generation to generation.

> Priest: Bless, ✠ O Lord, these *arras*
> that N. and N. will give to each other
> and pour over them the abundance of your good gifts.

> **Groom, then bride, presenting the coins to the other:**
> N., receive these *arras* as a pledge of God's blessing
> and a sign of the good gifts we will share.

HYMN OR CANTICLE OF PRAISE (NEW)

Although this hymn or canticle is an option, its inclusion provides an opportunity to involve the people more fully in this rite. This is not a solo; it is sung by all. No example is given. Any song or hymn that gives praise and thanksgiving to God is appropriate.

The possibilities for selections are numerous — a setting of the Magnificat, a hymn (e.g., "Praise God from Whom All Blessings Flow"), or a Psalm of praise (e.g., Psalm 104 — This is the day the Lord has made ...). The song should have a familiar melody or an easy refrain. Composers are encouraged to prepare music for this.

In some parts of the country, the bride and groom kiss at this point. There is no invitation given in the rite for the Priest to invite this action. A priest may be inclined to invite the assembly to applaud at this moment. Applause is a popular cultural response of affirmation at both private and public occasions. However, it is not really a liturgical response. During the applause there can, at times, be added shouts of congratulations, which may sound culturally appropriate, but may not be liturgically appropriate or necessary. A sung response is better suited to this moment; it directs the response in a specific manner to what God is doing in the lives of this couple.

THE UNIVERSAL PRAYER

The Universal Prayer is to be offered in the usual manner. The person who normally speaks the petitions is the Deacon or a Reader. The ordering and focus of these prayers are somewhat different from the petitions of a Sunday liturgy (GIRM 69). The petitions during a Ritual Mass may be more specific to the occasion (GIRM 70).

Two examples of the Universal Prayer are given in the Appendix to *The Order of Celebrating Matrimony* (OCM 216-217). These examples do not preclude that the petitions may be composed for the wedding. With guidance on form and content, the couple may write the intercessions — seeking God's assistance for their own marriage, for their family members, for all married couples, for the poor and the needy, for families everywhere, and for the dead, perhaps the bride and groom's deceased family and friends.

THE CREED

The liturgical day may prescribe the recitation of the Creed. If the wedding takes place on a Sunday or a Solemnity, the Creed or "Symbol" is said according to the rubrics. "Symbol" is another word for Creed — the word, "*symbolon*" (Greek) refers to an authoritative list of doctrine. This word also refers to the distinctive mark of those who hold this belief.

Unlike Sunday, the Creed follows the Universal Prayer in the Ritual Mass. In this way, the petitions stay closer to the actual exchange of Consent as we pray for the couple who just spoke that Consent.

THE LITURGY OF THE EUCHARIST

POSTURE, PLACEMENT, AND MINISTERS

The Rite presumes that at the conclusion of the Rite of Marriage any of the witnesses who were standing near the newly married couple have returned to their places after the Universal Prayer.

What does the Rite say about the placement and posture of the newly married couple during the Preparation of the Gifts? It does not say anything, other than "the Bride and Groom, when appropriate, may bring the bread and wine to the altar" (OCM 70). This would imply that the couple may be seated and then stand to go to the place where the bread and wine are located. The bread and wine are then brought forward by the bride and groom to the priest who will take them. The couple would return to their places, again to be seated.

If the bride and groom prefer, other people may bring up the gifts — perhaps parents, grandparents, godparents, other members of the family, or friends. This option offers the opportunity to involve others in the liturgy. These same people should also be eligible to receive Holy Communion.

Having the couple stand during the Preparation of Gifts is unnecessary and only invites photo opts from the assembly. The bride and groom would assume the same posture as the rest of the assembly.

THE EUCHARISTIC PRAYER

In many churches, the bride and groom go to a kneeler within the sanctuary for the *Eucharistic Prayer*. The Marriage Rite does not indicate where the couple's placement should be. It is assumed that the couple would have the same posture as the liturgical assembly during the Eucharistic Prayer. It is not recommended that they stand or be seated during the Eucharistic Prayer. These postures do not facilitate participation nor respect for the ritual action.

In the 1969 edition, a "Commemoration of the Couple" was provided for Eucharistic Prayer I (The Roman Canon). This embolism is also provided in *The Order of Celebrating Matrimony, second edition*. A new translation of the proper form of the *hanc igitur* appears in at OCM 71A. This already had been included in *The Roman Missal, third edition* (2011) in the "Ritual Mass V: For the Celebration of Marriage." The words in parentheses may be omitted if the occasion so suggests.

Therefore, Lord, we pray:
graciously accept this oblation of our service,
the offering of your servants N. and N.
and of your whole family,
who entreat your majesty on their behalf;
and as you have brought them to their wedding day,
so (gladden them with your gift of the children they desire and)
bring them in your kindness
to the length of days for which they hope.
(Through Christ our Lord. Amen.)

In the 2016 edition, a "Commemoration of the Couple" has now been provided for Eucharistic Prayers II and III (see OCM 203 and 204). Again, these have already been available since the promulgation of the English translation of *The Roman Missal, third edition.*

In Eucharistic Prayer II   *after the words "… and all the clergy."*
Be mindful also, Lord, of N. and N.,
whom you have brought to their wedding day,
so that by your grace
they may abide in mutual love and in peace.

In Eucharistic Prayer III   *after the words "… whom you have summoned before you."*
Strengthen, we pray, in the grace of Marriage N. and N.,
whom you have brought happily to their wedding day,
that under your protection
they may always be faithful in their lives
to the covenant they have sealed in your presence.
In your compassion, O merciful Father,
gather to yourself all your children
scattered throughout the world.

OPTIONAL: THE BLESSING AND PLACING OF THE *LAZO* OR THE VEIL

The second approved cultural adaptation is the "The Blessing and Placing of the *Lazo* or the Veil" (71b). This, too, was chosen because of its antiquity. This adaptation was included in the 2010 Spanish translation of the *Ritual del Matrimonio* for use in the dioceses of the United States. While this tradition is mostly found in Hispanic cultures, no one may be prohibited from using this approved cultural adaptation. If included, this rite takes place before the Nuptial Blessing.

In some cultures it is customary to use the *lazo* (or *lasso*). It may be a garland of flowers, a cord, or resemble a large rosary (or two rosaries intertwined). It symbolizes the unification of the husband and wife for the rest of their lives.

A veil may also be used in addition to (or in place of) the garland/cord/beads. It may be a separate veil or it may be the bride's veil, extended over the shoulders of the groom. Occasionally, the symbols are combined — the couple might use a veil which has one edge decorated with a cord or garland of flowers. The symbol(s) are traditionally brought forward by family members or friends, often the godparents.

"If the *lazo* has not been placed earlier, and it is now convenient to do so, it may be placed at this time or else a veil is placed over the head of the bride and the shoulders of the husband" (OCM 71B) The *lazo* and/or veil are in place during the Nuptial Blessing. There is no directive on when the *lazo* or veil are removed.

THE LORD'S PRAYER

Next, the Lord's Prayer is sung/recited. The prayer, *Deliver us ...* is omitted and the invitation to the Nuptial Blessing follows.

THE NUPTIAL BLESSING

The Nuptial Blessing follows the Lord's Prayer. The current placement of the Nuptial Blessing is one of the last remaining vestiges of what at one time was a flexible and adaptive part of the Mass in the tradition of the Gelasian *Sacramentaries*. However, it is properly linked to the Eucharistic Prayer; indeed, it contains an invocation to the Father to send down the Holy Spirit, similar to the epiclesis of the Eucharistic Prayer.

The Nuptial Blessing is not to be omitted (OCM 72) in the celebration of Matrimony within Mass or the celebration of Matrimony without Mass. (It may be omitted in *The Order of Celebrating Matrimony between a Catholic and a Catechumen or a Non-Christian* [OCM 138]. In this case, a prayer is substituted in place of the Nuptial Blessing [OCM 140].)

There are three options for the Nuptial Blessing. The first is found, in place, within Chapter One (OCM 73-74). The chant notations for the Nuptial Blessings are found in Chapter IV (OCM 204-209). Their very presence encourages the presider to chant the text.

Priest: Dear brothers and sisters,   OCM 73
            let us humbly pray to the Lord
            that on these servants of his,
            now married in Christ,
            he may mercifully pour out
            the blessing of his grace
            and make of one heart in love
            (by the sacrament of Christ's Body and Blood)
            those he has joined by a holy covenant.

            Silent Prayer

            O God, who by your mighty power   OCM 74
            created all things out of nothing,
            and, when you had set in place
            the beginnings of the universe,
            formed man and woman in your own image,
            making the woman an inseparable helpmate to the man,
            that they might no longer be two, but one flesh,
            and taught that what you were pleased to make one
            must never be divided;

            O God, who consecrated the bond of Marriage
            by so great a mystery
            that in the wedding covenant you foreshadowed
            the Sacrament of Christ and his Church;   *cont.*

O God, by whom woman is joined to man
and the companionship they had in the beginning
is endowed with one blessing
not forfeited by original sin
nor washed away by the flood.

Look now with favor on these your servants,
joined together in Marriage,
who ask to be strengthened by your blessing.
Send down on them the grace of the Holy Spirit
and pour out your love into their hearts,
that they may remain faithful in the Marriage covenant.
May the grace of love and peace
abide in your daughter N.,
and let her always follow the example of those holy women
whose praises are sung in the Scriptures.

May her husband entrust his heart to her,
so that, acknowledging her as his equal
and his joint heir to the life of grace,
he may show her due honor
and cherish her always
with the love that Christ has for his Church.

And now, Lord, we implore you:
may these your servants
hold fast to the faith and keep your commandments;
made one in the flesh,
may they be blameless in all they do;
and with the strength that comes from the Gospel,
may they bear true witness to Christ before all;
(may they be blessed with children,
and prove themselves virtuous parents,
who live to see their children's children).

And grant that,
reaching at last the fullness of years for which they hope,
they may come to the life of the blessed in the Kingdom of Heaven.
Through Christ our Lord.
R. Amen.

BEST PRACTICE

When Marriage is celebrated within Mass, the rubric indicates that the couple can approach the altar or remain in their place and kneel (OCM 72). The Priest faces the couple, preferably standing in front of them, with hands extended.

With the Invitation, the Priest speaks first to the liturgical assembly (OCM 73). This text, as well as the Nuptial Blessing, is also found in *The Roman Missal, third edition at Ritual Mass V.* A moment of silence allows all to pray silently before the blessing is given and sufficient time should be given to permit the assembly to pray.

Then for the Blessing, the Priest is to extend both hands over the bride and bridegroom. This implies that someone else will hold the ritual book for the Priest.

This posture and placement gives the Priest and assembly a collaborative stance toward the couple, particularly since the assembly has been invited by the Priest "to humbly pray to the Lord that on these his servants, now married in Christ ..." (OCM 73).

The focus of the Nuptial Blessing is the action of God at work in the lives of all married couples. These texts no longer direct the blessing mainly to the bride alone. The Nuptial Blessing is more clearly directed to both the bride and the groom. It is God who creates, who consecrates, who joins. The Blessing given is to strengthen the man and woman to remain faithful, to do their own part in living out their promises, bearing witness through their marriage vows to the fruitfulness of the married state, including the procreation of children, until they reach the eternal life of Heaven.

As in the 1969 *Rite of Marriage,* the revised OCM points out that some words may be omitted in the Invitation if one of the spouses will not be receiving Communion. Likewise, the words in parentheses toward the end of the Nuptial Blessing may be omitted if the bride and groom are advanced in years.

THE SIGN OF PEACE

There are no rubrics in the OCM indicating how a gesture of peace is to be given. The bride and groom may offer a Sign of Peace to one another or immediate family. At times some brides and grooms want to extend the sign of peace and charity to their parents and give their parents a token, such as a rose. There is no provision in the Rite to indicate that giving of any token is to be done. However, it makes sense that offering the Sign of Peace to those nearby would include the couple's parents.

> There follows the Rite of Peace, by which the Church entreats peace and unity for herself and for the whole human family, and the faithful express to each other their ecclesial communion and mutual charity before communicating in the Sacrament. As for the actual sign of peace to be given, the manner is to be established by the Conference of Bishops in accordance with the culture and customs of the peoples. However, it is appropriate that each person, in sober manner, offer the sign of peace only to those who are nearest (GIRM 82).

> ... The priest may give the sign of peace to the ministers but always remains within the sanctuary, so that the celebration is not disrupted. In the diocese of the United States of America, for a good reason, on special occasions (for example, in the case of a funeral, a wedding or when civic leaders are present), the Priest may offer the Sign of Peace to a small number of the faithful near the sanctuary ... (GIRM 154).

Perhaps the best way to guide a request for an addition to the rite at this point is to ask the bride and groom what they believe the purpose of the Rite of Peace is? The cultural pull here is very strong for some kind of interaction to occur between the couple and their parents. Help the couple expand their understanding to see this action as more than a meet and greet, and to make it a liturgical act of offering peace and charity in the name of Christ to each other. New in their vocation, they share that same peace and charity to all others through their marriage. Good pastoral care would suggest that the couple be kindly told that this Sign of Peace and charity not overtake the liturgy honoring the liturgy's rhythmic flow.

Music should not be played during the Sign of Peace (SL 187).

HOLY COMMUNION

As usual, the Breaking of the Bread is accompanied by the Lamb of God litany.

Rightfully, the Introduction to the OCM names the reception of Holy Communion as one of the main elements of the celebration of Marriage.

> The main elements of the celebration of Marriage are to stand out clearly, [including] ... Eucharistic Communion of both spouses and of others present, by which, above all, their charity is nurtured and they are raised up to communion with the Lord and with their neighbor (OCM 35).

> If Marriage is celebrated within Mass, ... there should also be prepared ... a chalice of sufficient size for Communion under both kinds (OCM 38).

Distributing Holy Communion under both kinds is encouraged as it is a fuller expression of Eucharistic life. The 1969 ritual edition stated that the married couple may receive Communion under both kinds (RM 36). The revised edition of the OCM extends that permission to more Catholics:

> The bride and bridegroom, their parents, witnesses and relatives may receive Communion under both kinds (OCM 76).

For this to happen appropriately and reverently, the Priest who is presiding must adequately prepare any Extraordinary Ministers of Holy Communion who may be needed for the Communion Rite. This is particularly true if these ministers are not familiar with the church building's physical space. It would also be advantageous for the parish to provide the Extraordinary Ministers of Holy Communion needed for a wedding as part of parish service. Should the bride and groom serve as Extraordinary Ministers at their own wedding? This is not recommended. Rather, this gives the opportunity for others to serve in a ministry capacity. There is also concern that if the bride and groom serve as Extraordinary Ministers of Holy Communion, it could become a receiving line for best wishes.

Pastorally, the reception of Holy Communion at a wedding can be somewhat disconcerting. The liturgical assembly may be composed of people of other religious faiths or no particular religious belief; they may not be familiar at all with Catholic practice regarding Holy Communion. The second typical edition of the OCM states:

> Although pastors are ministers of Christ's Gospel for all, they should, nonetheless, direct special attention to those, whether Catholics or non-Catholics, who never or rarely take part in the celebration of Marriage or the Eucharist. This pastoral norm applies in the first place to the spouses themselves (OCM 37).

Should something be announced about the reception of Holy Communion? This is a delicate issue. The best solution may be to say simply and kindly, "Those who are Catholic and are receiving Holy Communion are invited to come forward and those who are not Catholics are invited to spend this time in prayer." Perhaps a simple, gracious statement could appear in the worship aid. The intent is to allow people to be better informed about our theology and practice and to be made more comfortable. When delivered correctly, it will be received in the spirit offered. In this celebration of the union of two families, it might be appropriate to speak of our hope of one day finding unity among those of different faith traditions. This kind of invitation can open doors for later dialogue.

What should the bride and groom be doing during the Communion Procession? After their own reception of the Sacrament, it is best if the bride and groom are not in a position to face the assembly. Encourage the bride and groom to sing and to pray with the assembly during the Communion Procession. What is expected of the liturgical assembly is expected of them.

The Prayer after Communion is taken from the "Ritual Mass V: For the Celebration of Marriage" or from the Mass of the Day, if the liturgical day does not permit the use of the Ritual Mass.

THE CONCLUSION OF THE CELEBRATION

The Priest greets the people in the usual way, as at all Masses.

The Solemn Blessing is offered (OCM 77). There is no option for a simple blessing. The Priest directs the first three invocations to the couple, with his hands extended over them. The Priest shifts his attention to all present for the final invocation. Additional options may be found in Chapter Four, Part IX — "Blessings at the End of the Celebration" (OCM 213-215).

Priest:	May God the eternal Father keep you of one heart in love for one another, that the peace of Christ may dwell in you and abide always in your home.
All:	Amen.
Priest:	May you be blessed in your children, have solace in your friends, and enjoy true peace with everyone.
All:	Amen.
Priest:	May you be witnesses in this world to God's charity, so that the afflicted and needy who have known your kindness may one day receive you thankfully into the dwelling of God.
All:	Amen.
Priest:	And may almighty God bless all of you, who are gathered here, the Father, and the Son, ✠ and the Holy Spirit.
All:	Amen.

THE LITURGICAL PROCESSION

The revised OCM is silent on how the recessional is to form. There is no directive for a closing hymn (there is none in the GIRM for any Mass). There is no rubric for how the ministers, Priest, couple, and witnesses are to leave the church.

Given what was said about a liturgical procession for the Entrance, a best practice would be to echo what was done in the entrance procession:

- Cross Bearer
- Bride and Groom together
- Witnesses
- Parents
- Servers
- [Assisting Deacon]
- Priest

SIGNING THE MARRIAGE RECORD

States have different requirements regarding who signs the license. In some states, only the officiant signs; in others, only the bride and groom; in still others, the officiant and the two witnesses. This is a civil document.

The revised OCM has a new rubric (a similar rubric appears in Chapters Two and Three):

> When the Mass is concluded, the witnesses and the Priest sign the Marriage record. The signing may take place either in the vesting room or in the presence of the people; however, it is not to be done on the altar (OCM78).

While this signing may be done in the presence of the assembly, such a gesture immediately brings the liturgy to a stop and makes the assembly spectators to the signing of a civil document. It elevates a legal signature to a greater dignity than it requires or deserves. The sacramental union has already taken place.

CHAPTER SIX:
About *The Order of Celebrating Matrimony Without Mass*

The Introductory Rites

- Greeting of the Bride and Groom
  (or after the procession)
- Entrance Procession
- Entrance Song
- Sign of the Cross
- Greeting of the People
- Introduction
- Collect

The Liturgy of the Word
- First Reading
- Responsorial Psalm
- Second Reading
- Gospel Acclamation
- Gospel
- Homily

The Celebration of Matrimony
- Address to the Bride and Groom
- The Questions before the Consent
- The Consent
- The Reception of the Consent
- The Blessing and Giving of Rings
- [The Blessing and Giving of the *Arras*]
- [Hymn or Canticle of Praise]
- The Universal Prayer (Prayer of the Faithful)
- The Lord's Prayer
- [The Blessing and Placing of the *Lazo* or the Veil]
- Nuptial Blessing

The Conclusion of the Celebration
- Simple Blessing
- [Song]
- The Recessional

The *Order of Celebrating Matrimony without Mass* is selected if a)the Marriage is between a Catholic and a baptized non-Catholic; b) a Priest is not available to celebrate Mass on the day selected; or c) pastoral circumstances suggest that celebrating this Sacrament during Mass would be not be appropriate for an assembly which may be predominantly non-Catholic. The rite itself provides the reasons why *The Order of Celebrating Matrimony without Mass* would be chosen.

> The celebration itself of the Sacrament must be diligently prepared, as far as possible, with the engaged couple. Marriage should normally be celebrated within Mass. Nevertheless, with due regard both for the necessities of pastor care and for the way in which the prospective spouses and those present participate in the life of the Church, the pastor should decide whether it would be preferable to propose that Marriage be celebrated within or outside of Mass (OCM 29).

> If a Marriage takes place between a Catholic and a baptized non-Catholic, the rite of Celebrating Matrimony without Mass should be used (OCM 79-117). If, however, the situation warrants it, the rite of Celebrating Matrimony within Mass (OCM 45-78) may be used, with the consent of the local Ordinary; but with regard to admission of the non-Catholic party to Eucharistic Communion, the norms issued for various cases are to be observed (OCM 36).

"When Mass is not celebrated, either by necessity or because of circumstances, the order described here is used, even by a Deacon" (OCM 79; see also OCM 24). These rubrics are new and the first mentions of the Deacon as a possible presider in *The Order of Celebrating Matrimony without Mass*. Indeed, Chapter Two of the OCM now uses the terms "priest or deacon" or "presider."

Paragraph 80 of the OCM provides directives for the proper vesture for this rite. The Priest is to wear "an alb or surplice, and a white or festive stole, and even a cope of the same color." A Deacon is to wear "an alb, a white or festive stole and a dalmatic."

THE INTRODUCTORY RITES

The comments give in this Pastoral Companion in the section on *The Order of Celebrating Matrimony within Mass* generally apply to this rite as well. There is no Penitential Act and, since this is not a Mass, there will be no Gloria.

GREETING OF THE BRIDAL PARTY (OCM 80, 84)

There are two forms for greeting the bridal party. If there is to be an entrance procession, the Priest or Deacon greets the bride, groom, parents, and attendants at the entrance of the church. If there will not be a liturgical procession, the presider and servers wait for them in sanctuary and he greets them when they arrive at their place.

THE ENTRANCE PROCESSION AND ENTRANCE SONG (OCM 81-82, 85)

Likewise, there are two options for the entrance procession. In the first form, the presider and other ministers have greeted the bridal party at the entrance of the church and all participate in the entrance procession.

Catholics begin their liturgies with processions, so, ideally, there should be a procession which looks familiar to us. Its order could be similar to the one suggested for *The Order of Celebrating Matrimony within Mass.*

- Cross bearer
- Servers
- Readers
- Presider
- Bridesmaids and Groomsmen
- Maid/Matron of Honor and Best Man
- Bride and Groom (three options for entry)
    Bride and Groom together
    Groom with parents; Bride with parents
    Groom; then Bride

In the second form, the presider stands in the sanctuary and awaits the bridal party. After he has greeted the couple, he reverences the altar with a profound bow, venerates it with a kiss, and goes to the chair (OCM 85). Meanwhile, the Entrance Chant takes place.

In either case, there is to be an Entrance Song in which the entire assembly participates.

SIGN OF THE CROSS/ GREETING OF THE PEOPLE

The Presider makes the Sign of the Cross and greets the people as at Mass.

INTRODUCTION

The presider greets the people using one of the two introductory addresses provided or may use "similar words." These are the same texts as provided in Chapter One (OCM 52-53). The first is addressed to the entire assembly; the second option is addressed to the couple.

Presider:	We have come rejoicing into the house of the Lord	OCM 87
	for this celebration, dear brothers and sisters,	
	and now we stand with N. and N.	
	on the day they intend to form a house of their own.	
	For them this is a moment of unique importance.	
	So let us support them	
	with our affection,	
	with our friendship,	
	and with our prayer as their brothers and sisters.	
	Let us listen attentively with them	
	to the word that God speaks to us today.	
	Then, with the holy Church,	
	let us humbly pray to God the Father,	
	through Christ our Lord,	
	for this couple, his servants,	
	that he lovingly accept them,	
	bless them,	
	and make them always one.	

<u>OR</u>

Presider: N. and N., the Church shares your joy   OCM 88
             and warmly welcomes you,
             together with your family and friends,
             as today,
             in the presence of God our Father,
             you establish between yourselves a lifelong partnership.
             May the Lord hear you on this joyful day.
             May he send you help from heaven and protect you.
             May he grant you your hearts' desire
             and fulfill every one of your prayers.

COLLECT

The presider now prayers the Opening Prayer or Collect as provided in the rite (OCM 89; also 190)

Presider: Be attentive to our prayers, O Lord,
             and in your kindness,
             pour out your grace on these your servants (N. and N.),
             that, coming together before your altar,
             they may be confirmed in love for one another.
             Through Christ our Lord.

All: Amen.

Alternately, the presider may use any of six collects supplied in Chapter IV (OCM 188, 189, 190, 191, 192, 193). Please be advised that if the presider has chosen the first option for the Nuptial Blessing, he should not choose the Collect found at OCM 188. The texts are redundant.

THE LITURGY OF THE WORD (OCM 90-91)

READINGS

The Liturgy of the Word would be the same as *The Order of Celebrating Matrimony within Mass*. There may be three readings (two readings and the Gospel reading) or there may be two readings (one reading and a Gospel reading).

One reading which explicitly speaks of marriage should be chosen — these are marked with an asterisk (OCM Chapter IV, nos. 144-187).

HOMILY

"The minister in the Homily uses the sacred text to expound the mystery of Christian Marriage, the dignity of conjugal love, the grace of the Sacrament, and the responsibilities of married people, keeping in mind, however, the various circumstances of individuals" (OCM 91). As in any good homily, he might draw on the Scriptures, the euchology of the ritual, or the texts of the rite itself. Indeed, the Introduction, especially nos. 1-11, provides a bounty of quotations deserving of theological reflection.

The recitation of the Creed is not included in this rite.

The ritual elements of *The Order of Celebrating Matrimony without Mass* are the same as the celebration within Mass (Cf. the commentary on pages XX- XX herein). Both cultural adaptations — The Blessing and Giving of *Arras* and The Blessing and Placing of the *Lazo* or the Veil — have been included in place (OCM 101B and 103B, respectively).

- Address to the Bride and Groom
- The Questions before the Consent
- The Consent
- The Reception of the Consent
- The Blessing and Giving of Rings
- [The Blessing and Giving of the *Arras*]
- [Hymn or Canticle of Praise]
- The Universal Prayer (Prayer of the Faithful)
- The Lord's Prayer
- [The Blessing and Placing of the *Lazo* or the Veil]
- The Nuptial Blessing

The Address to the bride and groom is the same as the celebration within Mass (OCM 93). The Questions before the Consent are also the same, as is the rubric that the third question may be eliminated if the couple is elderly or for other pastoral circumstances (OCM 94). The words of Consent (OCM 95-97) are the same — two options for the text and two methods for proclaiming them — in a declarative form or interrogatory form.

Similarly, there are two forms for the Reception of the Consent, including the new second option with its rich biblical imagery (OCM 98). The minister invites the assembly to praise God with the same new acclamation (OCM 99).

Presider:	Let us bless the Lord.
All:	Thanks be to God.

Another acclamation may be sung or said.

The Blessing and Giving of Rings follows (OCM 100, 194, or 195) with an optional sprinkling with holy water. The bride and groom exchange rings, with slightly new words — "receive this ring," instead of "take this ring ..."

Groom, then Bride:
> N., receive this ring
> as a sign of my love and fidelity.
> In the name of the Father, and of the Son,
> and of the Holy Spirit.

The Blessing and Giving of the *Arras* may follow (OCM 101B).

Then the assembly offers prayers for the couple and other marriage-related issues in the Universal Prayer (examples are provided in OCM nos. 216-217). If Holy Communion is not distributed, the Lord's Prayer follows (as it does in the Liturgy of the Hours). The concluding prayer is omitted and the presider proceeds to the Nuptial Blessing.

If the cultural adaptation of The Blessing and Placing of *Lazo* or the Veil (OCM 103b) has been chosen, the family brings forth the *lazo* and/or veil at this point, so that these symbols are in place for the Nuptial Blessing.

The couple remains in place and kneels (OCM 104); there is no reference to a movement toward the altar. The presider sings or says the Invitation to the Nuptial Blessing (OCM 104 and 105; see also 73, 206, 207, 208, 209). With hands extended over the bride and groom, he prays;

Let us humbly invoke God's blessing
upon this bride and groom,
that in his kindness he may favor with his help
those on whom he has bestowed the Sacrament of Matrimony.

OCM 104
text with music 205A

Silent Prayer

O God, who by your mighty power
created all things out of nothing,
and, when you had set in place
the beginnings of the universe,
formed man and woman in your own image,
making the woman an inseparable helpmate to the man,
that they might no longer be two, but one flesh,
and taught that what you were pleased to make one
must never be divided;

OCM 105
text with music 205B

O God, who consecrated the bond of Marriage
by so great a mystery
that in the wedding covenant you foreshadowed
the Sacrament of Christ and his Church;

O God, by whom woman is joined to man
and the companionship they had in the beginning
is endowed with one blessing
not forfeited by original sin
nor washed away by the flood.

Look now with favor on these your servants,
joined together in Marriage,
who ask to be strengthened by your blessing.
Send down on them the grace of the Holy Spirit
and pour out your love into their hearts,
that they may remain faithful in the Marriage covenant.
May the grace of love and peace
abide in your daughter N.,
and let her always follow the example of those holy women
whose praises are sung in the Scriptures.

May her husband entrust his heart to her,
so that, acknowledging her as his equal
and his joint heir to the life of grace,
he may show her due honor
and cherish her always
with the love that Christ has for his Church.

And now, Lord, we implore you:
may these your servants
hold fast to the faith
and keep your commandments;
made one in the flesh,
may they be blameless in all they do;
and with the strength that comes from the Gospel,
may they bear true witness to Christ before all;
(may they be blessed with children,
and prove themselves virtuous parents,
who live to see their children's children).

And grant that,
reaching at last the fullness of years for which they hope,
they may come to the life of the blessed in the Kingdom of Heaven.
Through Christ our Lord.
R. Amen.

The Nuptial Blessing is never omitted at a celebration within Mass or without Mass.

CONCLUSION OF THE CELEBRATION

A simple blessing immediately follows and the celebration comes to a swift conclusion.

May almighty God bless all of you gathered here,
the Father, and the Son, ✠ and the Holy Spirit.
R: Amen.

Unlike the celebration within Mass, there is a mention of a concluding song. "It is a praiseworthy practice to end the celebration with a suitable chant" (OCM 107).

THE ORDER OF CELEBRATING MATRIMONY WITHOUT MASS — WITH THE DISTRIBUTION OF HOLY COMMUNION

The *Order of Celebrating Matrimony without Mass* includes an alternate order when Holy Communion will be distributed. This practice would not be normative, but if the bride and groom are both Catholic and the decision to celebrate this Sacrament without Mass was made for good reason (perhaps a priest was not available), distributing Holy Communion is an option. However, in most cases, the reasons that the Sacrament of Matrimony is being celebrated without Mass would suggest that distribution of Holy Communion may not be the best decision. Some diocesan policies may prohibit this addition; please check with your chancery.

In the 1969 version of the *Rite of Marriage*, the texts of the Ordinary of the Mass were included. In the latest edition, those texts have been eliminated. It was assumed that the presider would have *The Roman Missal* at hand. However, in Chapter Two of the OCM, the presider's texts for the Rite of Distributing Holy Communion outside Mass have been included for ease of use.

If Holy Communion will be distributed, the Celebration of Matrimony would follow this order after the Liturgy of the Word:

- Address to the Bride and Groom (93)
- The Questions Before the Consent (94)
- The Consent (95-97)
- The Reception of the Consent (98)
- Acclamation (99)
- The Blessing and Giving of Rings (100-101)
- [The Blessing and Giving of the *Arras*] (101B)
- [Hymn or Canticle of Praise] (102)
- The Universal Prayer (including the presider's concluding prayer)
- [The Blessing and Placing of the *Lazo* or Veil] (103B)
- The Nuptial Blessing (104-105 or other)
- Holy Communion
  - Placement of the Reserved Sacrament on the altar (108)
  - Lord's Prayer (109)
  - Sign of Peace (110)
  - Invitation to Communion/Response of the Assembly (111)
  - Distribution of Holy Communion (112)
  - A suitable chant during the distribution of Holy Communion (113)
  - Period of Silence, Psalm or a Canticle of Praise sung by the assembly (114)
  - Prayer (115)
- The Conclusion of the Celebration
  - Final Blessing (116, 213-216)
  - Recessional Song or Instrumental Music

SIGN OF PEACE

The Sign of Peace expresses peace, charity, and unity, just before we share in the great Sacrament of unity. Ideally, this should not be a prolonged exchange; often it is appropriate to offer a sign of peace to immediate family members only.

DISTRIBUTION OF HOLY COMMUNION

If Holy Communion is to be distributed, it is done so after the Nuptial Blessing. The presider "approaches the place where the Eucharist is reserved, takes the vessel or ciborium with the Body of the Lord, places it on the altar and genuflects" (OCM 108). Since this is not a Mass, Communion is distributed under the species of bread alone.

THE COMMUNION HYMN

The assembly should sing during the Communion Procession (113). Many songs used during the distribution of Holy Communion at Mass are not appropriate for distribution outside Mass. For example, the text should not refer to the Body and Blood of Christ since Communion will be under the form of bread alone. Nor would the song include lyrics which refer to the offering we have just made to the Father.

PERIOD OF SILENT PRAYER

Aware of the great Sacrament they have received, the assembly should participate in a period of silent prayer.

PRAYER AFTER COMMUNION

The presider concludes the Communion Rite by offering a special prayer to God the Father.

> **Presider:**   Let us pray.
>
> Having been made partakers at your table,
> we pray, O Lord,
> that those who are united by the Sacrament of Marriage
> may always hold fast to you
> and proclaim your name to the world.
> Through Christ our Lord.
>
> R. Amen.

CONCLUSION OF THE CELEBRATION

If Holy Communion has been distributed, one would conclude with a Solemn Blessing (OCM 213-215). Again, it is commendable to conclude the entire celebration with a song.

It would not be appropriate to "introduce the couple for the first time as 'Mr. and Mrs. ...'" nor would it be appropriate to invite the groom to kiss his bride. The liturgy should conclude with the same dignity with which it began — a liturgical procession. The signing of the license may take place in the vesting room or in the presence of the people, but not on the altar (OCM 117).

CHAPTER SEVEN: About *The Order of Celebrating Matrimony Between a Catholic and a Catechumen or a Non-Christian*

[The Rite of Reception]

- Greeting of the Couple
- Entrance Procession
- Introduction

The Liturgy of the Word
- First Reading
- Responsorial Psalm
- [Second Reading]
- Gospel Acclamation
- Gospel
- Homily

The Celebration of Matrimony
- The Address
- The Questions before the Consent
- The Consent
- The Reception of the Consent
- [The Blessing and Giving of Rings]
- [The Blessing and Giving of the *Arras*]
- [Hymn or Canticle of Praise]
- The Universal Prayer (Prayer of the Faithful)
- The Lord's Prayer
- [The Blessing and Placing of the *Lazo* or the Veil]
- Nuptial Blessing or prayer (OCM 140)

The Conclusion of the Celebration
- Simple Blessing
- Song/Chant
- Recessional

If a Marriage takes place between a Catholic and an unbaptized person, *The Order of Celebrating Matrimony Between a Catholic and a Catechumen or a Non-Christian* (OCM 118-143) is to be used. The presider and couple may not choose the texts in Chapter One nor Chapter Two of *The Order of Celebrating Matrimony*.

The proper minister of this rite is a Priest or a Deacon who has received delegation from the local Ordinary or the pastor to assist at the celebration of Matrimony:

> With regard to Marriage, it is by no means rare for special cases to arise: such as Marriage with a baptized non-Catholic, with a catechumen, with a person who is simply unbaptized, or even with a person who has explicitly rejected the Catholic faith. Those in charge of pastoral care should keep in mind the norms of the Church pertaining to these types of cases, and they should, if the occasion requires, have recourse to the competent authority (OCM 22).

THE RITE OF RECEPTION

There is only one form given for the Rite of Reception. Its intention is to begin the celebration with a warm and dignified welcome. There is no prescribed text for this reception/greeting, but the instructions note that the presider greets the bridal party "warmly" (119).

> "At the appointed time, the Priest or Deacon, wearing an alb and stole, and even a cope (or a dalmatic, for a Deacon) of the color white or a festive color, goes with the servers to the door of the church or to the place that has been chosen, where he receives the bridal party and warmly greets them ..." (OCM 119).

This greeting is not delivered into a microphone. The Priest or presiding Deacon is addressing only the bridal party.

After this greeting, the one who presides, the servers, the couple, the witnesses, and all present go to the seats prepared for each one (119). It envisions a simple procession or movement to the seats which have been prepared. Ideally, the rite should take place in a Catholic church, however, it may be held in another suitable place. Check with your chancery for local policies and proper dispensations.

When all have reached their places, the presider addresses the couple. Using the names of the bride and groom, the presider asks them to prepare inwardly for the celebration of Marriage (120). The text, based on the text in the 1969 edition, is specific to this rite.

Presider:	N. and N., the Church shares your joy
	and warmly welcomes you,
	together with your families and friends,
	as today you establish between yourselves
	a lifelong partnership.
	For believers God is the source of love and fidelity,
	because God is love.
	So let us listen attentively to his word,
	and let us humbly pray to him,
	that he may grant you your heart's desire
	and fulfill every one of your prayers.

If circumstances so suggest, the Rite of Reception is omitted and the celebration of Marriage begins with the Liturgy of the Word (121). This would presume that participants are already in their places and that there has been some kind of greeting to the assembly. The greeting offered above (or similar words) might be spoken before the Liturgy of the Word begins.

THE LITURGY OF THE WORD

The Liturgy of the Word is celebrated in the usual manner with texts taken from those provided in OCM 144-187. One or two readings may be chosen. However, even one reading is permitted. At least one reading that explicitly speaks of Marriage must always be chosen (OCM 122).

THE CELEBRATION OF MATRIMONY

The Celebration of Matrimony follows the same form as *The Order of Celebrating Matrimony without Mass* with a few exceptions.

THE ADDRESS TO THE BRIDE AND GROOM

"With all standing, including the couple and the witnesses who are positioned near them " (OCM 124), the presider addresses the couple in these or similar words:

> Presider: Dearly beloved,
> you have come together here before a minister of the Church
> and in the presence of the community
> so that your intention to enter into Marriage
> may be strengthened by the Lord with a sacred seal,
> and your love be enriched with his blessing,
> so that you may have strength
> to be faithful to each other forever
> and to assume all the responsibilities of married life.
> And so, in the presence of the Church,
> I ask you to state your intentions.

THE QUESTIONS BEFORE THE CONSENT

The presider questions them about their freedom of choice, fidelity to each other, and the acceptance and upbringing of children. The content of the questions is the exact same as those found in Chapter One and Two of *The Order of Celebrating Matrimony*. Similarly, the third question can be eliminated if the couple is elderly or if some other pastoral circumstance would suggest it.

The bride and groom answer individually — "I have," "I am," and "I am."

THE CONSENT

The presider invites them to declare their consent. The text of the Consent is the same as in the other rites, and there are two methods for proclaiming them — declarative and interrogatory. No other words may be used for the Consent.

THE RECEPTION OF THE CONSENT

The presider receives their Consent with the same two options as provided in the other two rites (see page 63 herein). The new text, rich with Biblical imagery may be especially appropriate for some couples who will be celebrating their marriage using this rite.

The same acclamation is to be sung/recited by the presider and assembly: " Let us bless the Lord" and "Thanks be to God."

[THE BLESSING AND GIVING OF RINGS]

In this rite, The Blessing and Giving of Rings may be omitted. For example, perhaps some religions might not permit the wearing of jewelry. If it is included, the presider blesses the rings using the text provided in OCM nos. 131, 194, or 195.

When placing the ring on the finger of his/her spouse, the non-Christian may omit "In the name of the Father, and of the Son, and of the Holy Spirit" (OCM 132).

[THE BLESSING AND GIVING OF THE *ARRAS*]

There is an option to include the approved cultural adaptation of The Blessing and Giving of the *Arras* (OCM 133). The presider blesses the coins, then, the groom and bride give them to each other. Again, these are not only a sign of their financial support of each other, but also of the gifts they will share with those in need.

[HYMN OR CANTICLE OF PRAISE]

A hymn of canticle of praise may be sung by the whole community.

UNIVERSAL PRAYER

Now the entire assembly prays with and for the couple. Samples of the invitation and invocations are provided in the Appendix of the OCM (216-217). The concluding prayer is omitted, since the Lord's Prayer will immediately follow.

THE LORD'S PRAYER

In this rite, the Lord's Prayer is sung/recited by all Christians. This is made evident by the special invitation of the presider. It may be helpful to print this rubric and the full text of the prayer in a worship aid.

> Presider: God the Father wills that his children be of one heart in charity;
> let those who are Christian call upon him
> in the prayer of God's family,
> which our Lord Jesus has taught us.
>
> *And all the Christians continue:*
> Our Father, who art in heaven ...

[THE BLESSING AND PLACING OF THE *LAZO* OR THE VEIL]

According to local customs, the rite of blessing and the imposition of the *Lazo* (wedding garland) or of the veil may take place before the Nuptial Blessing" (OCM 137). The item(s) are brought forward by godparents, family or friends. The spouses remain at their place and kneel. The *lazo* is placed and/or the veil is placed over the head of the wife and the shoulders of the husband, thus symbolizing the bond that unites them (137).

THE NUPTIAL BLESSING

In the *Order of Celebrating Matrimony between a Catholic and a Catechumen or a Non-Christian*, there is only one option for the text of the Nuptial Blessing. The words reflect on the natural bond, not the sacramental bond.

The Invitation concludes with the words "the bond of Marriage" whereas invitations in the prevous chapters concluded with "the bond of Matrimony."

Presider:	Now let us humbly invoke God's blessing upon this bride and groom, that in his kindness he may favor with his help those on whom he has bestowed the bond of Marriage.	OCM 138

All pray in silence for a while.

Presider:	Holy Father, maker of the whole world, who created man and woman in your own image and willed that their union be crowned with your blessing, we humbly beseech you for these your servants, who are joined today in the Marriage covenant.	OCM 139 *chant OCM 209*

May your abundant blessing, Lord,
come down upon this bride, N.,
and upon N., her companion for life,
and may the power of your Holy Spirit
set their hearts aflame from on high,
so that living out together the gift of Matrimony,
they may be known for the integrity of their conduct
(and be recognized as virtuous parents).

In happiness may they praise you, O Lord,
in sorrow may they seek you out;
may they have the joy of your presence
to assist them in their toil,
and know that you are near
to comfort them in their need;
and after a happy old age,
together with their circle of friends that surrounds them,
may they come to the Kingdom of Heaven.
Through Christ our Lord.
R. Amen.

If circumstances suggest it, the Nuptial Blessing may be omitted, and the following prayer is spoken over the bride and bridegroom:

> Presider: Be attentive to our prayers, O Lord,
> and in your kindness uphold
> what you have established for the increase of the human race,
> so that the union you have created
> may be kept safe by your assistance.
> Through Christ our Lord.
> R. Amen

THE CONCLUSION OF THE CELEBRATION

SIMPLE BLESSING

The only option is for a simple blessing over all the people (OCM 141).

> Presider: May almighty God bless all of you, who are gathered here,
> the Father, and the Son, ✠ and the Holy Spirit.

SONG

"It is a praiseworthy practice to end the celebration with a suitable chant" (OCM 142).

SIGNING OF THE MARRIAGE RECORD

"When the celebration is concluded, the witnesses and the one who presides sign the Marriage record. The signing may take place either in the vesting room or in the presence of the people; however, it is not done on the altar" (143).

CHAPTER EIGHT:
The Appendix to *The Order of Celebrating Matrimony*

In the 1969 edition of the Rite of Marriage, there were two items in the Appendix. First, one would have found "Instructions on Communion Under Both Kinds" taken from the General Instruction to the Roman Missal (sic.) nos. 240-252. These would have been drawn from the first edition of the *Missale Romanum* (1969).

Second, one would have found "Homiletic Notes for the New Readings." These provided brief commentaries on readings from the Old Testament, New Testament, and the Gospel passages from Matthew, Mark, and John.

The 1991 edition (and its 2016 English translation) has eliminated both those documents. Instead, the second edition has three very helpful resources in its Appendix.

I.   Examples of the Universal Prayer
II. The Order of Blessing an Engaged Couple
III. The Order of Blessing a Married Couple within Mass on the Anniversary of Marriage

I. EXAMPLES OF THE UNIVERSAL PRAYER (OCM 216-217)

The rite provides two examples of the Universal Prayer (Prayer of the Faithful) that may be used for the wedding liturgy. The presider and couple may use them directly, adapt them for their use, or compose similar petitions especially for the day and pastoral circumstances.

At most celebrations of the Eucharist, the usual pattern should be followed: "for the needs of the Church, for public authorities and the salvation of the whole world; for those burdened by any kind of difficulty; for the local community" (GIRM 69-70). In any particular celebration of a Ritual Mass, such as a Marriage, "the series of intentions may be concerned more closely with the particular occasion" (GIRM 70).

Specific intentions may be included for the bride and groom, their families, as well as for the wider church. The individual invocations should be consistent with the Nuptial Blessing, yet not duplicate it (103A). They should be concise, easy to comprehend, and sensitive to those in the assembly. The invitation, invocations, and concluding prayer may be recited or sung (GIRM 69, SL 171).

One of the samples, Universal Prayer II, follows (OCM 217):

Presider:	Dear brothers and sisters, let us accompany this new family with our prayers, that the mutual love of this couple may grow daily and that God in his kindness will sustain all families throughout the world.
Reader:	For this bride and groom, and for their well-being as a family, let us pray to the Lord.
Assembly:	Lord, we ask you, hear our prayer.
Reader:	For their relatives and friends, and for all who have assisted this couple, let us pray to the Lord. R.
	For young people preparing to enter Marriage, and for all whom the Lord is calling to another state in life, let us pray to the Lord. R.
	For all families throughout the world and for lasting peace among all people, let us pray to the Lord. R.
	For all members of our families who have passed from this world, and for all the departed, let us pray to the Lord. R.
	For the Church, the holy People of God, and for unity among all Christians, let us pray to the Lord. R.
Presider:	Lord Jesus, who are present in our midst, as N. and N. seal their union accept our prayer and fill us with your Spirit. Who live and reign for ever and ever.
Assembly:	Amen.

II. THE ORDER OF BLESSING AN ENGAGED COUPLE

- Introduction (nos. 218-221)
- The Introductory Rites
  - Sign of Cross
  - Greeting
  - Introduction
- Reading of the Word of God (choose one of four)
  - John 15:9-12
  - 1 Corinthians 13:4-13
  - Hosea 2:21-26
  - Philippians 2:1-5
- Psalm 145: 8-9, 10 and 15, 17-18 Reflection
- Prayers
  - Invitation
  - Invocations
- [A Sign of Promise]
  - [Blessing of engagement rings]
- Prayer of Blessing
- Conclusion of the Rite
  - Blessing
  - Song

The Blessing of an Engaged Couple is a new translation/adaptation of the blessing found in the *Book of Blessings*, Chapter I.

INTRODUCTION

The text provides a lovely introduction on the "honorable betrothal of Christians ..." It notes that this celebration must be adapted to suit particular circumstances (218). "When the engagement is celebrated within the confines of the two families, one of the parents may appropriately preside at the rite of blessing.

If a Priest or Deacon is present, however, then the office of presiding more appropriately belongs to him, provided that it is clear to those present that the rite is not a celebration of Marriage itself" (219). "The order supplied here, therefore, may be used either by the parents, or by a Priest, a Deacon, or another layperson" (220). Some distinct texts and rubrics are provided when the presider is a lay person.

This rite may also be used when engaged couples are gathered together for catechetical preparation or for an engaged couples' weekend. This blessing is never combined with Mass.

INTRODUCTORY RITES

If a Priest or a Deacon presides, after the Sign of the Cross is made, then an appropriate greeting is used (222) or a greeting from the Roman Missal.

If the minister is a layperson, after the Sign of the Cross has been made, he or she greets those present, using the introduction in the rite (223). An introductory address follows (224).

> Presider: We know that God's grace is a constant need
> for everyone, at all times.
> Yet no one can doubt
> that members of God's faithful have special need of that grace
> when they are preparing to form a new family.
> And so, let us ask God's blessing
> upon our brother and sister (N. and N.),
> that they may grow in mutual respect,
> love each other more truly,
> and approach the celebration of holy Matrimony chastely
> through appropriate companionship and prayer together.

READING OF THE WORD OF GOD

One of those present or the minister reads a text of Sacred Scripture (225-227). The rite provides four selections, printed out in their entirety. Then Psalm 145 may be sung or said [or another suitable liturgical song] (228).

REFLECTION

"The one who presides may briefly address those present, shedding light on the biblical reading, so that they may understand with faith the meaning of the celebration and may be able to distinguish it correctly from the celebration of Marriage" (229).

PRAYERS

From the intercessions provided in the rite, the presider may select those that seem more suitable or may add others that apply to particular circumstances (230).

SIGN OF PROMISE

In accord with local customs, before the prayer of blessing, the engaged couple may express some sign of their promise to each other, by signing a document, or by the giving of rings or other gifts (231). The engagement rings or gifts may be blessed with the formula found in OCM 232.

> **Presider:** Safeguard the gifts you have exchanged,
> so that you may fulfill in due time
> the pledge you have offered each other.
> R. Amen.

PRAYER OF BLESSING

The presider, if a parent or other layperson, says the prayer with hands joined (233). If, however, the presider is a Priest of Deacon, the prayer is said with hands extended (233 or 234).

> **Presider:** We give you praise, O Lord,   OCM 233
> who in your gentle wisdom
> call and prepare your son and daughter N. and N.
> to love each other.
> Graciously strengthen their hearts, we pray,
> so that, by keeping faith and pleasing you in all things,
> they may come happily to the Sacrament of Marriage.
> Through Christ our Lord. Amen.
>
> *Or if the presider is a Priest or Deacon*
>
> Lord God, wellspring of all love,   OCM 234
> N. and N. have met each other
> through your providential plan.
> Mercifully grant as they seek your grace
> in preparing for the Sacrament of Marriage,
> that, sustained by heavenly ✠ blessing,
> they may grow in mutual respect
> and may love each other with true charity.
> Through Christ our Lord.
> R. Amen.

CONCLUSION OF THE RITE

The presider concludes the rite with a simple blessing (235).

Presider: May the God of love and peace
             dwell within you,
             direct your steps,
             and strengthen your hearts in his love.

All: Amen.

"It is a praiseworthy practice to conclude with a suitable chant" (236).

III. THE ORDER OF BLESSING A MARRIED COUPLE WITHIN MASS ON THE ANNIVERSARY OF MARRIAGE

- Introductory Rites
- Liturgy of the Word
  - First Reading
  - Responsorial Psalm
  - [Second Reading]
  - Gospel Verse
  - Gospel
  - Homily
- Renewal of Commitment (240-242)
  - Introduction
  - Renewal of Commitment (quietly of publicly)
  - Prayer of Thanksgiving
  - Concluding Prayer by the Presider
- The Blessing of Rings
  - Current rings (243)
  - or new rings (244 or 194)
- Universal Prayer (OCM 245)
  - Invitation
  - Invocations
  - Concluding Prayer
- Liturgy of the Eucharist
  - (As at Mass)
  - Lord's Prayer
  - Prayer of Blessing (248)
  - Sign of Peace (249)
  - Holy Communion (250)
- Concluding Rite
  - Solemn Blessing (251)

This blessing is a new translation and adaptation of the blessing found in Chapter I of the *Book of Blessings*. "On the main anniversaries of Marriage, as for example, on the twenty-fifth, fiftieth, or sixtieth anniversary, it is fitting to hold a special remembrance of the Sacrament by means of the celebration of the proper Mass with the prayers indicated in *The Roman Missal*" (237). Mass propers may be taken from *The Roman Missal*, Masses for Various Needs and Occasions #11: "On the Anniversaries of Marriage."

THE LITURGY OF THE WORD

Readings may be taken from *The Lectionary for Mass*, nos. 801-805 — "For the Celebration of Marriage" or nos. 943-947 "Mass for Giving Thanks to God." The Homily is based on the sacred text, keeping in mind the various circumstances of individuals.

The Order of Blessing begins after the reading of the Homily.

THE RENEWAL OF COMMITMENT

Please note that there is no "renewal of vows." This is unfortunate language which has crept into our lexicon over the years. It is neither necessary nor appropriate to "renew vows." One might argue that we renew baptismal promises each year; indeed it is appropriate to do so. One might even contend that priests renew their commitment to their Bishop annually at the Chrism Mass; indeed, texts are provided to do so. However, in neither of those instances is one repeating the actual matter and form of the sacrament. At Baptism, one is baptized with the pouring of water and the use of the Trinitarian formula. At Ordination, one receives the sacrament with the Laying on of Hands and the Prayer of Ordination. In the Sacrament of Marriage, the words of Consent actually do confer the sacrament; the bride and groom are the ministers of the sacrament. These words of Consent are permanent.

So, take note of the verbiage which the Church uses in this rite. The husband and wife "renew their commitment" by publicly thanking God for his blessings.

First, the Priest invites the couple to pray in silence and to renew before God their commitment to live their marriage in holiness (240).

The couple renews their commitment quietly or, if the couple, taking circumstances into account, wish to renew their commitment publicly, the following form is used (241-242):

> **Husband:**   Blessed are you, Lord,
> for by your goodness I took N. as my wife.
>
> **Wife:**   Blessed are you, Lord,
> for by your goodness I took N. as my husband.

Husband and Wife:

> Blessed are you, Lord,
> for in the good and bad times of our life
> you have stood lovingly by our side.
> Help us we pray,
> to remain faithful in our love for one another
> so that we may be true witnesses
> to the covenant you have made with humankind.

Priest:

> May the Lord keep you safe all the days of your life.
> May he be your comfort in adversity
> and your support in prosperity.
> May he fill your home with his blessings.
> Through Christ our Lord.

All:

> Amen.

Blessing of Rings

The rings they have are acknowledged in prayer and may be incensed (243). If new rings are presented, a distinct prayer of blessing is provided (OCM 244, 194).

Universal Prayer (Prayer of the Faithful)

The Order of Blessing provides an invitation, invocations, and a concluding prayer (OCM 245-246). These may be adapted for the occasion and the liturgical season.

THE LITURGY OF THE EUCHARIST

The Liturgy of the Eucharist is celebrated as usual. The husband and wife may bring up the bread and wine at the Presentation of the Gifts.

Prayer of Blessing

This prayer of blessing echoes some of the same sentiments as the Nuptial Blessing at a wedding liturgy. But this prayer acknowledges what God has already done for them in their married life.

After the Our Father, "Deliver us ..." is omitted. The Priest faces the couple with extended hands and prays for them, using the text in OCM 248.

Presider: We praise you, O God,
we bless you, Creator of all things,
who in the beginning made man and woman
that they might form a communion of life and love.
We also give you thanks
for graciously blessing the family life
of your servants N. and N.,
so that it might present an image of Christ's union with the Church.
Therefore look with kindness upon them today,
and as you have sustained their communion
amid joys and struggles,
renew their Marriage covenant each day,
increase their charity,
and strengthen them in the bond of peace,
so that (, together with the circle of their children that surrounds them,)
they may forever enjoy your blessing.
Through Christ our Lord.

All: Amen.

Sign of Peace

In accord with local custom the couple and all others may offer one another a sign that suitably expresses peace and charity (249).

Holy Communion

The couple may receive Communion under both kinds (250). In many dioceses the Bishop has already given permission for all the faithful to receive Communion under both kinds as indicated in the General Instruction of the Roman Missal (GIRM 223).

THE CONCLUDING RITE

Solemn Blessing

The text for a solemn blessing, particular to this occasion, is provided at OCM 251.

Deacon:	Bow down for the blessing.
Priest:	May God the all-powerful Father grant you his joy.
All:	Amen.
Priest:	May the Only Begotten Son of God stand by you with compassion in good times and bad.
All:	Amen.
Priest:	May the Holy Spirit always pour forth his love into your hearts.
All:	Amen.
Priest:	And may almighty God bless all of you, who are gathered here, the Father, and the Son, ✠ and the Holy Spirit.
All:	Amen.

PART IV

Music and the Wedding Liturgy

CHAPTER NINE:
Music and the Wedding Liturgy

THE PARISH MUSIC DIRECTOR AND PASTORAL CARE

The interaction of the parish music director with the bride and groom is an essential part of the Church's ministry to engaged couples. It presents opportunities for catechesis, evangelization, and pastoral care.

Before all else, we need to extend a warm welcome! Most couples come to our parishes with little formal knowledge of liturgy, even if they are "good practicing Catholics." Others have been away from regular church attendance for a while and will need some pastoral sensitivity.

Sing to the Lord: Music in Divine Worship reminds us that a person's wedding day should be filled with joy and grace (SL 216-224). First and foremost, the music director should represent the Church in a caring and loving manner and should show enthusiasm and support at the couple's decision to marry in the Church.

In his encyclical, *Evangelii Gaudium*, Pope Francis reminds us:

> "The Eucharist, although it is the fullness of sacramental life, is not a prize for the perfect but a powerful medicine and nourishment for the weak ... Frequently, we act as arbiters of grace rather than its facilitators. But the Church is not a tollhouse; it is the house of the Father, where there is a place for everyone, with all their problems" (EG 47).

Whatever the faith practices of the engaged couple, they are part of the Church and should be treated with respect and dignity. Taking the time to return their phone calls, replying to their emails and being patient with their questions go a long way in this effort.

The process of selecting music can be overwhelming for couples — they already have so many decisions to make for their wedding. While the parents of the bride and/or groom often have the best of intentions when they call to discuss the music or try to make requests on behalf of their children, parents do a disservice to the engaged couple if they make decisions for them. It would be helpful if pastors strongly urge that the church's ministers and staff deal solely with the bride and groom. It is important that both the bride and the groom make these decisions together.

Ideally a face-to-face meeting with the couple offers the best way to get to know the couple. Sometimes there are sessions with a group of couples, perhaps as part of the marriage preparation program. For couples that live a great distance from the parish, contact may have to be primarily by phone or email.

MUSIC SELECTIONS

How does one make the couple aware of appropriate repertoire so that they can be prepared to make informed decisions?

Many brides and grooms are influenced by what they saw and heard at a friend's wedding — which may or may not have been celebrated in a Catholic church. And, of course, internet searches suggest all kinds of "wedding songs." Therefore, it is important that we provide resources which will not only catechize the engaged couple, but also help them to embrace the holiness of the liturgical celebration. Perhaps the music director meets with them one-on-one. Perhaps he/she gathers engaged couples for a "demonstration" of wedding music and catechesis on the liturgy. Perhaps both the presider and musician have created a parish guideline with suggested hymnody (which should not be restrictive or exclusive). How often does music about God's gift of love enter the parish's repertoire so that it would become a "favorite" for couples?

It could be of some limited help to have musical recordings available to assist couples with the selection of music for their wedding. There are copyright issues that must be considered. Printing or providing recorded music without the permission of the copyright holder is not only a legal issue, but a moral one as well. Commercial wedding recordings are a concern since many of these are put together with orchestral music and do not take into account the fact that most churches have organs or pianos. Orchestral music played on the organ or piano simply will not sound the way it does on the recording and disappointment may well result. In addition, parish musicians have differing abilities and repertoires. They may not have access to the selections which were on the recordings.

WHERE TO BEGIN?

An important principle to keep in mind is that no one plans the liturgy. It plans us! The role of the music director is to help couples prepare their wedding liturgy. That means that the primary resources are *The Order of Celebrating Matrimony*, the *Lectionary for Mass* and *The Roman Missal*. Articles, websites, social media, workshops and even this Pastoral Companion are good secondary sources, but should be considered alongside the primary sources.

THE WORSHIP AID

Well-produced and well-constructed worship aids will greatly encourage the participation of the assembly, an assembly which is most likely made up of practicing and non-practicing Catholics, people from different parishes with different repertoire, and people from different faith traditions, different cultures and ethnicities, etc.

> Since the celebration of marriage is a communal celebration, participation aids should be provided to the congregation so that they might follow the ritual with understanding. This, in turn, allows them to have full and active participation in the celebration. Participation aids should include especially those elements of the Liturgy unique to the marriage rite, as well as translations of any songs not sung in the vernacular. Such participation aids should also include proper copyright notices for permission to use copyrighted music in the program"(Sing to the Lord: Music in Divine Worship, 224).

Such worship aids ought to include the names of the liturgical ministers, an outline of the order of service, the people's responses, any particular instructions that the assembly might need and a notation of where the hymns are located in the hymnal.

It is also appropriate to include the words and music of the hymns and acclamations, provided the appropriate copyright licenses have been secured. Most of the major publishers have annual reprint licenses which make it easier for parishes to report usage of reprinted music and lyrics. It is not necessary to reprint the full text of the readings and prayers, except if the liturgy will be bi-lingual. Worship aids ought to be beautiful and dignified, as befits the celebration of the Liturgy.

The music director should be involved in the preparation of worship aids if they are used for weddings. Even if the music director is not directly responsible for designing and printing the worship aid, he/she ought to at least approve it before it goes to print. The presiding minister should do so as well.

Among the resources which the FDLC has produced is *The Gift of Love: A Bride and Groom's Guide to Preparing the Wedding Liturgy*. It includes all necessary elements of the liturgy, people's parts, and proper vocabulary. It also provides helpful information on each of the three rites of Marriage.

DIOCESAN AND PARISH GUIDELINES

Diocesan and parish guidelines need to be clearly written so that certain expectations are delineated. When these guidelines have been implemented, they should be published on the parish website or printed in the bulletin. They might be part of a package given to the couple when they have their initial interview with their presider. Couples should also be given advance notice if any of the policies or guidelines change. Policies and guidelines are meant to be helpful to the parish and to the couple. They ought to be enforced consistently, however, not so rigidly that they preclude any conversation that may enlighten all involved.

There are times when the priest, deacon or music minister may deem it necessary to make an exception to a policy. The last canon in the 1983 *Code of Canon Law* states: "The supreme law of the Church is the salvation of souls." Saint Pope John Paul II once said: "Canon law is necessary and secondary. The Mysteries are primary." These are good reminders to Church ministers — to follow the law not only faithfully, but flexibly as they assist the couple in making their wedding day truly a day of great joy and a day of the manifestation of Christ's love for His Church. Sometimes the most pastoral response to a specific request has to be "no"; however, when "no" has to be said, it should be carefully explained. For instance, most couples are more understanding when they know why a particular piece of music is not allowed. It is also helpful to offer other alternatives to what they suggest if it is not suitable for the liturgy.

Parish guidelines should go hand in hand with those of the diocese and one should not be more restrictive than the other. Problems frequently arise when neighboring parishes have different policies that contradict each other, or when different clergy within the same parish interpret the guidelines differently.

MUSIC MINISTERS DURING THE WEDDING

The Cantor is both a singer and a leader of congregational song (SL 37). Ideally, the Cantor dialogues with the liturgical assembly. Within *The Order of Celebrating Matrimony*, there are times when the Cantor can assist the assembly, such as in leading the acclamation in the Reception of the Consent, or assist the assembly in a hymn or canticle of praise after The Blessing and Giving of Rings.

The cantor may serve as the psalmist leading the verses of the Responsorial Psalm. The cantor can intone and sing the verse of the Gospel Acclamation, sing the invocations of the Universal Prayer, and lead the chanting of the Lamb of God . The cantor may also sing the verses of the psalm or the hymn that accompanies the entrance procession, the Preparation of the Gifts and the Communion procession.

For some in the liturgical assembly, experiencing a skilled cantor as a leader of congregational song could be a new experience. Singing at a Catholic wedding has not been generally encouraged. As such, the cantor should take part entire gathered assembly. The voice of the Cantor is to assist, not dominate the Assembly's own voice.

> Vocalists may sing alone during the Preparation of the Gifts or after Communion, provided the music and their manner of singing does not call attention to themselves but rather assists in the contemplation of the sacred mysteries being celebrated. Soloists should not usurp parts of the Mass designated for congregational participation (SL 221).

When offering this ministry, the Cantor ought to be visible to the assembly and not hidden in a choir loft.

The organist or pianist also plays an important liturgical role at weddings. In addition to leading the assembly's song, the keyboardist accompanies the cantor on solo verses. He/she also sets the tone for the wedding by playing appropriate instrumental music, before, during and after the Liturgy. Such music could draw from the Church's treasury of sacred music handed down through the centuries by composers of various eras and cultures.

Many other instruments also enrich the celebration of the Liturgy, such as wind, stringed, or percussion instruments 'according to longstanding local usage, provided they are truly apt for sacred use or can be rendered apt' (SL 90).

Some couples may wish to make use of the services of musicians who are not part of the parish music staff. These might include family members or friends. The pastor and music director should take such requests into consideration, but ultimately, they should also be sensitive to good liturgical practices. The request for a cantor who sings regularly at another parish might be handled differently than someone who sings in a secular band and may not have experience with Catholic Liturgy. Couples should be encouraged to bring this request to the attention of the music director or pastor early on in the process. Likewise, the parish policy on guest musicians should be made clear from the beginning as well. The remuneration of the parish musician is another factor that must be taken into consideration, particularly when rehearsal time is needed with guest musicians.

How many of your parish musicians (or local talent) are placed at the service of weddings? Do couples know that parish cantors can serve at the wedding? Do family friends (trained or untrained) have to step in to do this on a Saturday afternoon? How can we "screen" volunteers or recruit more skilled musicians to serve at all our sacramental celebrations?

All musicians, whether they are part of the parish music staff or are friends or family members of the couple, should clearly understand their role which is to be ministers who use their gifts and talents to help the people give praise to God. Musicians are not there to dominate the action or entertain the liturgical assembly, but to lead them deeper into the Paschal Mystery.

RECORDED MUSIC AND SECULAR MUSIC

"The role of liturgical musicians is ministerial in nature and cannot be replaced by electronic means. Likewise, recorded music lacks the authenticity provided by a living liturgical assembly gathered for the Sacred Liturgy" (SL 93). Recorded music is not permitted at wedding liturgies; while it might be used at the wedding rehearsal, it is not to be used within the Liturgy.

Popular love songs and secular music, even though they may emphasize the love of the spouses for one another, are not appropriate for the Sacred Liturgy since they exclude God and the Church community. While they may say loving things, they often don't say enough about the Author of Love and God's ongoing role in a Christian Marriage. Such songs are better suited to the reception.

PRINCIPLES FOR CHOOSING MUSIC

Sing to the Lord: Music in Divine Worship (USCCB, 2007) echoed earlier documents ("Music in Catholic Worship" and "Liturgical Music Today"):

> The marriage Liturgy presents particular challenges and opportunities to planners. Both musicians and pastors should make every effort to assist couples to understand and share in the planning of their marriage Liturgy. Since oftentimes the only music familiar to the couple is not necessarily suitable to the sacrament, the pastoral musician will make an effort to demonstrate a wide range of music appropriate for the Liturgy" (SL, 218).

> The primary role of music in the Liturgy is to help the members of the gathered assembly to join themselves with the action of Christ and to give voice to the gift of faith (SL 125).

Liturgical music unites us with the action of Christ's suffering, death, resurrection and ascension, that Paschal Mystery that we encounter at the Church's liturgy. The texts that we sing at Liturgy echo what the Church believes and these texts must be able to bear the weight of the mysteries that we celebrate. There has to be a careful balance between music that speaks to our personal relationship to God and our relationship with the Church (i.e. with each other).

The suitability of texts sung at weddings is an important consideration, as the words sung in the liturgy should "... always be in conformity with Catholic doctrine. Indeed, they should be drawn chiefly from Sacred Scripture and from liturgical sources" (SC 121). The selection of music for the wedding liturgy is guided by the same norms as apply to the gathering of the Church on Sundays.

Sing to the Lord proposed **three judgments** which might be used together to form **one evaluation** for the choice of music (126-136).

The Liturgical Judgment

The nature of the liturgy itself will help to determine what kind of music is called for, what parts are to be preferred for singing, and who is to sing them. "A certain balance among the various elements of the Liturgy should be sought, so that less important elements do not overshadow more important ones. Textual elements include the ability of a musical setting to support the liturgical text and to convey meaning faithful to the teaching of the Church" (SL 128).

The Pastoral Judgment

This judgment takes into consideration the actual community gathered to celebrate in a particular place at a particular time. Liturgical assemblies are composed of people of many different nationalities, cultures and histories. People have their own musical tradition which greatly influences their religious and social life. For this reason their music should be held in proper esteem and a suitable place is to be given to it (SC 119). The deepest question remains: "Will this composition draw this particular people closer to the mystery of Christ, which is at the heart of this liturgical celebration" (SL 133)?

The Musical Judgment

This judgment asks whether this composition has the necessary aesthetic qualities that can bear the weight of the mysteries celebrated in the Liturgy. Is the music technically, aesthetically, and expressively worthy? "To admit to the Liturgy the cheap, the trite, the musical cliché often found in secular popular songs is to cheapen the Liturgy, to expose it to ridicule, and to invite failure" (SL 135).

In summary, suitable texts include those which 1) speak explicitly of the Christian, religious dimension of love; 2) express trust in, thanksgiving to, or praise to God; and 3) support the action of the liturgy (e.g., a Communion hymn during the Communion procession). Unsuitable texts include those which 1) explicitly deny the Christian dimension of love (e.g. texts that imply "my life has no meaning without you" or "life isn't worth living without you"); 2) fail to mention God (or only mention God by implication); or 3) only faintly allude to the Christian dimension of love with inspiring or consoling sentiments.

MUSIC IN SERVICE TO THE LITURGY

BEFORE THE LITURGY

Prelude

As the guests are being seated, it is appropriate for the musicians to play and/or sing appropriate prelude music to help set a festive atmosphere for the Liturgy. The assembly could be invited to sing along, or it could be an opportunity for a sung or instrumental solo, or both.

Rehearsal with the Assembly

It would be advisable for the cantor to have a brief rehearsal with the liturgical assembly before the procession begins. This affords the assembly an opportunity to learn any unfamiliar hymns, acclamations or responses. It also helps to quiet people down. Too often people's conversations get louder and louder as the church fills up with people. Getting their attention is a way to keep them focused on the holy event in which they are about to participate. The rehearsal need not be lengthy nor attempt to include every musical piece, maybe just one or two unfamiliar pieces.

THE INTRODUCTORY RITES

The Procession

The purpose of the Introductory Rites is to ensure that the faithful who have come together as one establish communion and dispose themselves properly to listen to the Word of God and to celebrate the Eucharist worthily (GIRM 46).

It is customary in most churches to have festive instrumental music played during the liturgical procession. There are many classical selections that are appropriate for the procession. A single piece of music for the entire procession is best. Many couples request a separate piece of music for the bride; however, that would not be respectful of the equal importance of the bride and groom. It is possible for the musicians to increase the volume and change the tempo for the bride and groom.

Before the processional begins, the cantor or another suitable minister could welcome everyone to the celebration, if that has not already been done. The assembly should be invited to stand for the entire procession.

Opening Hymn

The revised *Order of Celebrating Matrimony* mandates an Entrance Chant/ Song for the Opening Procession. The purpose of this entrance chant is the same as it is for the Sunday Liturgy. The Entrance Procession may be accompanied by instrumental music or a suitable song. If instrumental music has been played, the liturgical assembly can flow directly into the verses of the same hymn, once all have taken their places. (SL 222) One might also consider a refrain style hymn so that the assembly can both watch and sing during the procession.

Psalm 20, Psalm 90 and Psalm 145 are the appointed Entrance Antiphons from *The Roman Missal* for weddings. Alternately, a strophic hymn with a beautiful and appropriate text set to a familiar hymn tune could be used. To foster assembly singing at weddings, it is helpful to give them music that they are familiar with, particularly because there are often many guests from other parishes or even other faith traditions.

Glory to God

With the implementation of the Roman Missal, third edition, the *Glory to God* is to be *sung/said at all Ritual Masses, even on weekdays of Advent and Lent.*

It takes pastoral sensitivity to develop a repertoire of service music for the parts of the Mass. In addition, even though a musical setting may be one familiar to the parish for Sunday worship does not mean that the same setting may be applicable to singing at a wedding. Experience and time will help with the music director collect Mass settings which can be routinely at weddings.

THE LITURGY OF THE WORD

Responsorial Psalm

The Order for Celebrating Matrimony provides seven options of the *Responsorial Psalm* (OCM 167-173). It is best to use musical settings which are compatible with the translations found either in the *Lectionary for Mass* or in the OCM.

Just as at Sunday Mass, the psalmist or cantor should proclaim the psalm from the ambo or another suitable place (GIRM 61). If it is not sung from the ambo, it should at least be sung from a place where the cantor is visible to the assembly since the psalmist is engaging in a dialogue with the rest of the assembly.

Gospel Acclamation

The Gospel acclamation is always sung. There are four options for the verse (all from the First letter of John, chapter four). The verses are printed in *The Order for Celebrating Matrimony* (OCM 174-177). The Alleluia is the appropriate acclamation, except during Lent when another appropriate acclamation of praise is sung.

The revised OCM suggests a new Lenten acclamation — "Sing joyfully to God our strength" (Psalm 81:2).

THE CELEBRATION OF MATRIMONY

Acclamation After the Reception of Consent

The *Order for Celebrating Matrimony* suggests the acclamation "Let us bless the Lord" and its response "Thanks be to God." It is preferable to sing this acclamation and response since it follows a climactic moment in the rite.

It also allows that another acclamation be sung or said (OCM 65). This might be something that is rehearsed with the liturgical assembly ahead of time. An Alleluia response could also be used (outside of the Lenten Season), although if this is done, it would be advisable to use a different setting than was used during the Gospel Acclamation.

Hymn Or Canticle Of Praise

After the Blessing and Giving of Rings and the optional Blessing and Giving of the *Arras, The Order for Celebrating Matrimony* states: "Then a hymn or canticle of praise may be sung by the whole community" (OCM 68). It is clear from the phrase "may be sung" that this is optional. This is not time for a solo or instrumental music. This hymn or canticle should permit the whole assembly to express their thanks and praise to God. They have just witnessed the profound moment of two lives becoming one in Christ.

THE LITURGY OF THE EUCHARIST

Music at the Presentation of Gifts

"At the beginning of the Liturgy of the Eucharist the gifts which will become Christ's Body and Blood are brought to the altar … It is a praiseworthy practice for the bread and wine to be presented by the faithful … Once the offerings have been placed on the altar and the accompanying rites completed, by means of the invitation to pray with the Priest and by means of the Prayer over the Offerings, the Preparation of Gifts is concluded and preparation is made for the Eucharistic Prayer" (GIRM 73, 77). During this time, instrumental music may be played or a hymn may be sung by the assembly. If a solo is chosen for the wedding, this would be the time to do it in the Liturgy. The time required for this rite is usually brief since there is no monetary collection.

Acclamations and Chants

Just as at a Sunday liturgy , the acclamations during the Eucharistic Prayer (Holy, Holy, Holy, Memorial Acclamation and the Amen) should be sung. The *Lamb of God* litany during the Communion Rite is also sung using a familiar setting.

Communion Hymn

The *Communion Procession* is one of the major processions of the Mass. During this time, we sing as a sign of our unity on our journey to the altar to receive the sacrament of unity. The singing begins at the moment the priest first partakes of Holy Communion and continues until the last person receives. Music during the *Communion Procession* should always be appropriate to the action and should be Christocentric.

Devotional hymns which are better suited adoration of the Blessed Sacrament are usually not appropriate for the Communion Procession. The Communion hymn, or at least the refrain, should be something that the assembly can sing.

A responsorial form of singing, similar to the way we sing the Responsorial Psalm, is appropriate during the Communion Procession since the assembly is moving and singing at the same time. When sung outside the Liturgy of the Word, psalms may be arranged in a hymn setting. For example, Psalm 34:2, 9 (Taste and see the goodness of the Lord) is a Communion psalm *par excellence* and is one of the Communion Antiphons prescribed in *The Roman Missal*. The other Communion Antiphons might be Ephesians 5:25,27 (Husbands love your wives…) and John 13:34 (I give you a new commandment, love one another …).

THE CONCLUDING RITES

Closing Hymn

The Order for Celebrating Matrimony states "It is a praiseworthy practice to end the celebration with a suitable chant" (OCM 107). This is only mentioned in *The Order of Celebrating Marriage without Mass* not *within Mass*. That is because there is no "closing hymn" in the Order of Mass. But since most assemblies sing a hymn at the conclusion of Mass and during celebrations of the other sacraments, it might be appropriate to sing a hymn at the conclusion of the wedding.

Recessional Music

Recessional music may accompany the procession of the bride and groom, the bridal party, and the liturgical ministers. There are a number of festive instrumental pieces of music that would be appropriate at this time.

PART V

Other Considerations

CHAPTER TEN:
Maintaining the Integrity of the Rite

Over the course of years, there have been practices, additions, and gestures that have become common place at many Catholic weddings in the United States, but have never been part of the Catholic sacramental rite of Matrimony. These additions have been given meaning through family memories, through the perceived expression of love, or simply because it has been given various symbolic meanings.

Handling these requests needs pastoral care, kindness and a willingness to help a couple understand what they are asking for and why they are asking for it. Thus, dialogue about a practice could be an opportunity to broaden the couple's understanding about Catholic worship, to respect their cultural heritage, and to highlight the importance of God's love for them on their wedding day. Sometimes, this dialogue is not easy; some couples find it to be an open-ended invitation to invent repetitive ways to express love and unity. However, dialogue can result in a collaboration that respects the Catholic Marriage rite and deepens the couple's participation in that rite.

Balancing the tension between the liturgical law and the pastoral practice is seldom easy. Preserving the relationship between the Church ministers and the couple is important. However, wise counsel will lead to wise choices about ritually expressing what *getting* married and what *being* married means.

In truth, all of the following practices could be called *cultural* in that they reflect certain values about this current time, what it means to be family, what being married means. Some of them are obviously more popular in certain locales than in others. However, the United States Bishops have chosen to not include any of these in *The Order of Celebrating Matrimony*.

AN APPROACH: A COUPLE'S PRAYER BEFORE A STATUE OF THE BLESSED MOTHER

There are no provisions given in the revised *Order of Celebrating Matrimony* for this practice. However, in many parts of the country, this procession and prayer by the newly married couple before a statue of the Blessed Mother is requested at weddings.

If this tradition is requested by the bride and groom, simply ask "why?" In reality, if the couple has a devotion to the Blessed Mother, asking her intercession for the sake of the couple's marriage could be appropriate in the couple's private prayer, at the rehearsal or at the reception. However, if no such devotion exists, or the bride or groom is not Catholic, serious questions would need to be raised about the appropriateness of such an addition. Is this just a photo opportunity? Is this being done so *Ave Maria* could be sung during the wedding? Perhaps this action would be best considered in a simple prayer service at the end of the wedding rehearsal.

While prayer before a statue of the Blessed Mother is not the center of the wedding rite, this practice can hold strong family memories. In some places this practice is so strong that to prohibit it without any alternatives would cause consternation. Thus, try to deepen its meaning with catechesis and strategic placement. Within this *Pastoral Companion* there is a sample prayer service — "A Couple's Prayer before a Statue of the Blessed Mother." It could be used to close a rehearsal. In this way, both families might be able to join in prayer and to seek Mary's intercession for the soon-to-be married couple.

AN APPROACH : THE UNITY CANDLE

There is a connection between Catholics and candles. Catholics light candles at Mass. They light them as extension of private prayer. The Paschal Candle is a symbol for Christ, the Light of the world; we bless it and light it to begin the great Easter Vigil. Candles can be carried in procession and are used during ritual prayer.

So why don't we use a so-called "unity candle" at a wedding? This practice is popular in some parts of the United States and not in others. At first look, it seems to be another expression of the couple's union, including a signal that the bride and groom come from their own unique families. This is symbolized by having the mother of the bride and the mother of the groom each light a side candle. In turn, after their vows, the newly married couple lights a single pillar candle from the two side candles; some say it represents becoming their own family. Often the bride and groom blow out the flames of the two side candles.

While this could be a laudable practice in itself, a closer look reveals possible problems. Again, ask the question "why?" If the couple has already expressed the words of Consent and has already exchanged wedding rings, what further signs of unity are needed? Did this practice come into common use because some ministers did not celebrate the Marriage ritual fully enough? One wonders why this ritual includes the mothers lighting candles. Could it be because the mothers are sometimes excluded from the Entrance Procession? One might also question which candles are used. Parents rarely use the bride and groom's baptismal candles, nor are the two side candles lit using the flame from the Paschal Candle. Upon lighting the Unity Candle, the newly-married couple usually extinguishes the side candles. What does that symbolize? Are they extinguishing their past or are they breaking their ties with their families of origin? The bride and groom do nothing with the remaining lit candle once they depart from the wedding. No mention is made of their bearing the light of Christ into the world through their Marriage.

While the unity candle strives to express the family identity of the engaged couple, their ties with their family histories, and their distinct memories, these expressions have already been made obvious. Both parents accompanying the bride and the groom in the Entrance Procession manifests this more eloquently.

Elsewhere in this *Pastoral Companion* it was said that there is a common desire to personalize the rituals we do: to make the rituals somehow expressive of one's unique self. Yet, within the Rite of Matrimony there are many opportunities to personalize the Marriage celebration so that the expression of a couple's unique love is celebrated. Another practice is not necessary. The lighting of the unity candle is simply not found in *The Order of Celebrating Matrimony*. Once again, the placement of this practice should not be included within the wedding ceremony. The addition or removal of parts of the Marriage ritual is not permitted.

The best place for this candle and its ritual would be at the rehearsal dinner or even at the reception after the wedding. Included in this *Companion* is a sample prayer service for such an occasion.

AN APPROACH : THE SANDS CEREMONY

There appears to be no limit to the creativity of the marketing world in discovering ways to promote some sort of visual expression of the realities of marriage: e.g., planting trees, colored waters, etc. Here is one more practice that is sometimes requested for a Catholic wedding.

It is very similar to the Unity Candle, only instead of using candles, the bride and groom use two vials of sand representing the "blending of families." As one advertisement states: "Sand ceremonies are especially appropriate for beach weddings but they may be used in any venue to enrich a brief exchange of vows or to create a lasting memento for the new couple."

This practice belongs at a rehearsal supper or reception. It is not part of the Catholic ritual for Matrimony. There are already many expressions of the couple's unique love within the Catholic ritual. A newly married couple does not really want a sand ceremony to be the lasting "memento" of a wedding. The exchange of vows and the sharing of rings speak of their unique love long after the sand has blown away.

If requested, offer the couple the enclosed prayer service for the unity candle which can be adapted for the sands and used at the reception.

AN APPROACH: JUMPING THE BROOM

This wedding practice appears to have its origins with the Romani people, especially in Wales, and has gained some popularity among African Americans. While the meaning of such a broomstick marriage in history referred to both legal and illegal marriages, finding a purpose and meaning today within a Catholic wedding can be difficult. Again, here is another sign of unity which attempts to repeat what is already within the Marriage rite — the Consent, the rings, and the blessings.

The practice of "jumping the broom" does express, as do other practices, a desire to remember the families of origin while creating a new family through this ritual act. Jumping the Broom also has a history in the African American community in that it carries a memory of slavery, injustices done to slaves, and of escape for those who wished to marry.

What to do? Since this gesture is often done at the end of the Marriage ceremony, it could be done after the couple leave the Church. However, the same questions about this practice would need to be asked as with the other additional practices: Why does the couple want this to be done? What meaning does it have for them both? What part of their personal history is prompting them to request this at the wedding? Can this gesture better be done at the reception?

IN SUMMARY

As pastors of souls, one must exercise great sensitivity when dealing with the varying requests to incorporate practices into the Marriage liturgy. It is good to remember that much of what is currently done within the liturgy grew from someone "adding" something to the basic liturgical rite. While not mentioned here, there may be other common place practices in specific locales now or which may develop over time. Use the same principles given above to determine if and how a requested practice is to be received and how one might respond.

PART VI

Helpful Resources

A Preparation Form for *The Order of Celebrating Matrimony within Mass*

Bride

Groom

Bride's Phone Number

Groom's Phone Number

Bride's Email Address

Groom's Email Address

Priest: _____

Date and Time of Wedding: _____

Time to Arrive at Church: _____

Date and Time of Rehearsal: _____

LITURGICAL MINISTERS

Deacon (optional): _____

Cross Bearer (optional): _____

Reader(s): _____

Reader of the Universal Prayer (Prayer of the Faithful): _____

Altar Servers: _____

Gift Bearers: _____

Extraordinary Ministers of Holy Communion: _____

Musicians: _____

Organist/Keyboardist: _____

Cantor: _____

Other Musicians: _____

Hospitality Greeters/Ushers: _____

Wedding Party: _____

Official witnesses: _____

Other attendants: _____

THE ENVIRONMENT FOR THE LITURGY

Church Contact Person: _____

Phone Number: _____ Email Address: _____

Person representing Bride and Groom for the Environment (Wedding Consultant, Florist, etc.):

_____

Phone Number: _____ Email Address: _____

Liturgical Season: _____

Placement of Flowers, Greenery, Candles etc.: _____

Parish Guidelines for the Liturgical Environment reviewed: ☐ YES ☐ NO

Special requests for the church environment: _____

_____

_____

Person(s) responsible to remove wedding items from the church environment after wedding:

_____

_____

| Photographer | Phone Number | Email Address |

_____

| Videographer | Phone Number | Email Address |

THE WEDDING LITURGY

Prelude Music: _____

_____

<u>The Introductory Rites</u>

Greeting of the Bride and Groom ☐ At the entrance ☐ At their place

Entrance Procession ☐ A ☐ B ☐ C

Music for the Procession: _____

Opening Song/Composer: _____

Sign of the Cross

Greeting of the People

Introduction ☐ A ☐ B ☐ Other

Glory to God ☐ Spoken ☐ Sung

Musical Setting: _____

Collect: _____

The Liturgy of the Word

First Reading: _____

Reader: _____

Responsorial Psalm: _____

Cantor: _____

Musical Setting: _____

Second Reading: _____

Reader: _____

Gospel Acclamation: _____

Setting: _____

Gospel: _____

Proclaimed by: _____

Homilist: _____

THE CELEBRATION OF MATRIMONY

Address to the Bride and Groom	Priest
Questions Before the Consent	Priest
The Consent	☐ Form A ☐ Form B ☐ Recited ☐ Question format
The Reception of Consent	☐ Form A ☐ Form B

Acclamation: _____

☐ Spoken ☐ Sung

The Blessing and Giving of Rings   ☐ Form A   ☐ Form B   ☐ Form C

[The Blessing and Giving of the *Arras*]   ☐ Cultural Adaptation   ☐ Omitted

Hymn or Canticle of Praise   ☐ Yes   ☐ Omitted

     Title/Composer: _____

The Universal Prayer   ☐ Model I   ☐ Model II   ☐ Composed

     Reader: _____

Profession of Faith   ☐ Omitted   ☐ Prescribed on this day

The Liturgy of the Eucharist

Presentation of the Bread and Wine: _____

Gift Bearers: _____

Eucharistic Prayer: _____

Preface: _____

Holy, Holy, Holy: _____

Mystery of Faith: _____

Amen: _____

Setting/Composer: _____

The Communion Rite

The Lord's Prayer   ☐ Recited   ☐ Sung

[Blessing and Placing of the *Lazo* or Veil]   ☐ Cultural Adaption   ☐ Omitted

Nuptial Blessing

     Introduction to the Blessing   ☐ Form A   ☐ Form B   ☐ Form C   ☐ Form D

     Silent Prayer

     Prayer of Blessing   ☐ Form A   ☐ Form B   ☐ Form C

Sign of Peace

Breaking of the Bread

     Lamb of God: _____

Communion Procession

     Song(s): _____

Prayer after Communion

THE CONCLUSION OF THE CELEBRATION

Solemn Blessing

Recessional   ☐ Instrumental   ☐ Song

Signing of the Marriage Record

A Preparation Form for *The Order of Celebrating Matrimony without Mass*

Bride   Groom

Bride's Phone Number   Groom's Phone Number

Bride's Email Address   Groom's Email Address

Priest: _____

Date and Time of Wedding: _____

Time to Arrive at Church: _____

Date and Time of Rehearsal: _____

LITURGICAL MINISTERS

Deacon (optional): _____

Cross Bearer (optional): _____

Reader(s): _____

Reader of the Universal Prayer (Prayer of the Faithful): _____

Altar Servers: _____

[Extraordinary Ministers of Holy Communion]: _____

Musicians: _____

Organist/Keyboardist: _____

Cantor: _____

Other Musicians: _____

Hospitality Greeters/Ushers: _____

Wedding Party: _____

Official witnesses: _____

Other attendants: _____

THE ENVIRONMENT FOR THE LITURGY

Church Contact Person: _____

Phone Number: _____ Email Address: _____

Person representing Bride and Groom for the Environment (Wedding Consultant, Florist, etc.):

_____

Phone Number: _____ Email Address: _____

Liturgical Season: _____

Placement of Flowers, Greenery, Candles etc.: _____

Parish Guidelines for the Liturgical Environment reviewed: ☐ YES   ☐ NO

Special requests for the church environment: _____

_____

_____

Person(s) responsible to remove wedding items from the church environment after wedding:

_____

_____

Photographer   Phone Number   Email Address

_____

Videographer   Phone Number   Email Address

THE WEDDING LITURGY

Prelude Music: _____

_____

The Introductory Rites

Greeting of the Bride and Groom   ☐ At the entrance   ☐ At their place

Entrance Procession   ☐ A   ☐ B   ☐ C

Music for the Procession: _____

Opening Song/Composer: _____

Sign of the Cross

Greeting of the People

Introduction   ☐ A   ☐ B   ☐ Other

Collect: _____

The Liturgy of the Word

First Reading: _____

Reader: _____

Responsorial Psalm: _____

Cantor: _____

Musical Setting and Composer: _____

Second Reading: _____

Reader: _____

Gospel Acclamation: _____

Setting: _____

Gospel: _____

Proclaimed by: _____

Homilist: _____

THE CELEBRATION OF MATRIMONY

Address to the Bride and Groom	Presider
Questions Before the Consent	Presider
The Consent	☐ Form A ☐ Form B ☐ Recited ☐ Question format
The Reception of Consent	☐ Form A ☐ Form B

Acclamation: _____

        ☐ Spoken   ☐ Sung

The Blessing and Giving of Rings   ☐ Form A   ☐ Form B   ☐ Form C

[The Blessing and Giving of the *Arras*]   ☐ Cultural Adaptation   ☐ Omitted

Hymn or Canticle of Praise   ☐ Yes   ☐ Omitted

      Title/Composer: _____

The Universal Prayer   ☐ Model I   ☐ Model II ☐ Composed

      Reader: _____

The Lord's Prayer   ☐ Recited   ☐ Sung

[Blessing and Placing of the *Lazo* or Veil]   ☐ Cultural Adaption ☐ Omitted

Nuptial Blessing

      Introduction to the Blessing   ☐ Form A   ☐ Form B   ☐ Form C   ☐ Form D

      Silent Prayer

      Prayer of Blessing   ☐ Form A   ☐ Form B   ☐ Form C

THE CONCLUSION OF THE CELEBRATION

Solemn Blessing

Recessional   ☐ Instrumental ☐ Song

Signing of the Marriage Record

After the Canticle of Praise...

The Universal Prayer   ☐ Model I   ☐ Model II   ☐ Composed

     Reader: _____

[Blessing and Placing of the *Lazo* or Veil]   ☐ Cultural Adaption   ☐ Omitted

Nuptial Blessing

     Introduction to the Blessing   ☐ Form A   ☐ Form B   ☐ Form C   ☐ Form D

     Silent Prayer

     Prayer of Blessing   ☐ Form A   ☐ Form B   ☐ Form C

The Lord's Prayer   ☐ Recited   ☐ Sung

Sign of Peace

Invitation to Communion   "Behold the Lamb of God..."

Disribution of Holy Communion

     Song: _____

Period after Communion   ☐ Silence   ☐ Psalm or Canticle of Praise

Prayer   OCM 115

THE CONCLUSION OF THE CELEBRATION

Blessing   ☐ Form A (Simple)   ☐ Form B (Solemn)
            ☐ Form C (Solemn)   ☐ Form D (Solemn)

Recessional   ☐ Instrumental   ☐ Song

Signing of the Marriage Record

A Preparation Form for *The Order of Celebrating Matrimony Between a Catholic and a Catechumen or Non-Christian*

Bride _____   Groom _____

Bride's Phone Number _____   Groom's Phone Number _____

Bride's Email Address _____   Groom's Email Address _____

Priest: _____

Date and Time of Wedding: _____

Time to Arrive at Church: _____

Date and Time of Rehearsal: _____

LITURGICAL MINISTERS

Deacon (optional): _____

Cross Bearer (optional): _____

Reader(s): _____

Reader of the Universal Prayer (Prayer of the Faithful): _____

Altar Servers: _____

Musicians: _____

Organist/Keyboardist: _____

Cantor: _____

Other Musicians: _____

Hospitality Greeters/Ushers: _____

Wedding Party: _____

Official witnesses: _____

Other attendants: _____

THE ENVIRONMENT FOR THE LITURGY

Church Contact Person: _____

Phone Number: _____ Email Address: _____

Person representing Bride and Groom for the Environment (Wedding Consultant, Florist, etc.):

_____

Phone Number: _____ Email Address: _____

Liturgical Season: _____

Placement of Flowers, Greenery, Candles etc.: _____

Parish Guidelines for the Liturgical Environment reviewed: ☐ YES   ☐ NO

Special requests for the church environment: _____

_____

_____

Person(s) responsible to remove wedding items from the church environment after wedding:

_____

_____

Photographer   Phone Number   Email Address

_____

Videographer   Phone Number   Email Address

THE WEDDING LITURGY

Prelude Music: _____

The Introductory Rites

Greeting of the Bride and Groom   ☐ At the entrance   ☐ At their place

Entrance Procession   ☐ A   ☐ B   ☐ C

Music for the Procession: _____

Introduction   ☐ OCM 120   ☐ Other

The Liturgy of the Word

First Reading: _____

Reader: _____

Responsorial Psalm: _____

Cantor: _____

Musical Setting and Composer: _____

Gospel Acclamation: _____

Setting: _____

Gospel: _____

Proclaimed by: _____

Homilist: _____

THE CELEBRATION OF MATRIMONY

Address to the Bride and Groom   Presider

Questions before the Consent   Presider

The Consent   ☐ Form A   ☐ Form B   ☐ Recited   ☐ Question format

The Reception of Consent   ☐ Form A   ☐ Form B

Acclamation: _____

     ☐ Spoken   ☐ Sung

The Blessing and Giving of Rings   ☐ Form A   ☐ Form B   ☐ Form C

[The Blessing and Giving of the *Arras*]   ☐ Cultural Adaptation   ☐ Omitted

Hymn or Canticle of Praise   ☐ Sung   ☐ Omitted

     Title/Composer: _____

The Universal Prayer   ☐ Model I   ☐ Model II   ☐ Composed

     Reader: _____

The Lord's Prayer   ☐ Recited   ☐ Sung

[Blessing and Placing of the *Lazo* or Veil]   ☐ Cultural Adaption   ☐ Omitted

Nuptial Blessing

     Introduction to the Blessing   OCM 138

     Silent Prayer

     Prayer of Blessing   OCM 139
     (OR)
     Prayer over the Bride and Groom   OCM 140

THE CONCLUSION OF THE CELEBRATION

Solemn Blessing

Recessional   ☐ Instrumental ☐ Song

Signing of the Marriage Record

A Prayer Service before a Statue of the Blessed Virgin Mary

This prayer service may be prayed at the conclusion of the wedding rehearsal .

The entire wedding party gathers in the front pews of the church. All stand. The priest, deacon or prayer leader begins:

INTRODUCTORY RITE

Leader: ✠ In the name of the Father, and of the Son, and of the Holy Spirit.

All: Amen.

Leader: God chose Mary to be the Mother of Jesus.
She was an obedient servant of the Lord
and always faithful to her call.
We praise God for calling us to be his disciples
and for calling us to this sacred vocation of Marriage.
Today [tonight] we seek the intercession of Mary, our Mother,
that _____and_____ will have a long, fruitful, and happy married life.
May Mary and her blessed spouse, Joseph,
help them to live a holy life as man and wife.

THE WORD OF GOD   Colossians 3:12-17

Reader: A reading from the Letter of Saint Paul to the Colossians

Brothers and sisters:
Put on, as God's chosen ones, holy and beloved,
      heartfelt compassion, kindness, humility, gentleness and patience,
      bearing with one another and forgiving one another,
      if one has a grievance against another;
      as the Lord has forgiven you, so must you also do.
And above all these things put on love,
      that is the bond of perfection.
And let the peace of Christ control your hearts,
      the peace into which you were called in one body.
And be thankful.
Let the word of Christ dwell in you richly,
      as in all wisdom you teach and admonish one another,
      singing psalms, hymns, and spiritual songs
      with gratitude in your hearts to God.
And whatever you do, in word or in deed,
      do everything in the name of the Lord Jesus,
      giving thanks to God the Father through him.

The word of the Lord.

(Taken from the Lectionary for Mass, no. 17, Feast of the Holy Family of Jesus, Mary, and Joseph)

Together, the couple goes to the statue of the Blessed Mother. They may bring a tribute of flowers. They remain there as long as they would like to pray.

They then return to stand in front of the leader who will conclude the prayer.

CONCLUDING PRAYERS

Leader: Let us pray.

All: Hail Mary…

Leader: God, send your blessing upon us
who celebrate the promised union of ___and ____.
May you bring to completion all that they hope for,
through the intercession of Mary,
the Mother of your Son.
Who lives and and reigns for ever and ever. Amen.

If a priest or Deacon is presiding:

Leader: The Lord be with you

All: And with your spirit.

BLESSING

Leader: May God fill us with joy at believing.

All: Amen.

Leader: May the peace of God reign in our hearts.

All: Amen.

Leader: May the Holy Spirit pour out his gifts upon us.

All: Amen.

Leader: Go in peace.

All: Thanks be to God.

A Prayer for the Lighting of a Unity Candle

This service may take place at the rehearsal dinner or at the wedding reception hall. A unity candle may be prepared on a small table. Matches and three tapers might be placed nearby.

The family and loved ones of the couple gather around them. The Leader begins.

INTRODUCTION

Leader: ✠ In the name of the Father, and of the Son, and of the Holy Spirit.

All: Amen.

Leader: Let us heed the words of St. Paul to the Romans: Romans 12: 2, 9-13

*Do not conform yourselves to this age
but be transformed by the renewal of your mind,
that you may discern what is the will of God,
what is good and pleasing and perfect.*

*Let love be sincere;
hate what is evil,
hold on to what is good;
love one another with mutual affection;
anticipate one another in showing honor.*

*Do not grow slack in zeal,
be fervent in spirit, serve the Lord.
Rejoice in hope,
endure in affliction,
persevere in prayer.
Contribute to the needs of the holy ones,
exercise hospitality.*

With these words to guide what we now do,
I would ask the parents of the bride and groom,
and the bride and groom to come forward
and stand before your family and friends.

LIGHTING OF THE PARENTS' CANDLES

Leader: We praise God for allowing us to celebrate the union of this couple
whom we love so much.
Let us pray in these words:
God is ever faithful.

All: *God is ever faithful.*

FOR THE GROOM

Leader: ___ and ___ , the parents of the bridegroom____,
cherish their son and their new daughter ___ .
They now light a candle to represent the light of Christ
which has guided their son to this day.

All: *God is ever faithful.*

FOR THE BRIDE

Leader: ___ and ___ , the parents of the bride____,
cherish their daughter and their new son ___
They now light a candle to represent the light of Christ
which has guided their daughter to this day.

All: *God is ever faithful.*

LIGHTING OF THE COUPLE'S CANDLE

After the parents have lit the two candles, the bride and groom come forward together to light the center candle using the two side candles. The Leader continues

Leader: ____and____now affirm their desire to become one in mind and heart,
grateful for the love, support and blessings
received from their families and friends.
May Christ's light continue to guide them in their married life,
brighten their way in times of darkness,
console them when the way is not clear,
and surround them with God's grace all the days of their married life.
We say again:

All: *God is ever faithful.*

CONCLUSION

Leader: And together we pray in the words our Savior gave us.

All: Our Father...

Leader: O God, you bless us here with family and friends.
May we celebrate your faithfulness in the lives of ___and ___ .
Allow us to be joyful in our expectations
that you will bring to fulfilment what you have begun.
We praise you now and forever and ever.

All: Amen.

INTRODUCTION TO *THE ORDER OF CELEBRATING MATRIMONY*

[1] Cf. C.I.C. can. 1055, §1.

[2] Cf. Second Vatican Council, Pastoral Constitution on the Church in the Modern World, Gaudium et spes, no. 48.

[3] Cf. ibid.

[4] Matthew 19:6.

[5] Cf. Nuptial Blessing.

[6] Cf. Second Vatican Council, Pastoral Constitution on the Church in the Modern World, Gaudium et spes, no. 48.

[7] Cf. 2 Corinthians 5:17.

[8] Cf. Matthew 19:6.

[9] Cf. Second Vatican Council, Pastoral Constitution on the Church in the Modern World, Gaudium et spes, no. 48.

[10] Ibid.

[11] Cf. John Paul II, Apostolic Exhortation, Familiaris consortio, no. 13: A.A.S. 74 (1982), 95; cf Second Vatican Council, Pastoral Constitution on the Church in the Modern World, Gaudium et spes, no. 48.

[12] Cf. C.I.C., can. 1055, '2.

[13] Cf. Ephesians 5:25.

[14] Cf. 1 Corinthians 7:7; Second Vatican Council, Dogmatic Constitution on the Church, Lumen gentium, no. 11.

[15] Cf. Ephesians 5:25.

[16] Cf. Second Vatican Council, Pastoral Constitution on the Church in the Modern World, Gaudium et spes, nos. 48, 50.

[17] Cf. ibid., no. 49.

[18] Cf. ibid., no. 50.

[19] Cf. 1 Corinthians 7:5.

[20] Cf. Second Vatican Council, Pastoral Constitution on the Church in the Modern World, Gaudium et spes, no. 50.

[21] Cf. John Paul II, Apostolic Exhortation, Familiaris consortio, no. 51: A.A.S. 74 (1982), 143.

[22] Tertullian, Ad uxorem, II, VIII: CCL I, 393.

[23] Cf. John Paul II, Apostolic Exhortation, Familiaris consortio, no. 66: A.A.S. 74 (1982), 159-162.

[24] Cf. ibid.; cf. C.I.C., can. 1063-1064.

[25] Cf. C.I.C., can. 1063.

[26] Cf. Second Vatican Council, Constitution on the Sacred Liturgy, Sacrosanctum Concilium, art. 59.

[27] Cf. C.I.C., can. 1065.

[28] Cf. ibid., can. 1066.

[29] Cf. John Paul II, Apostolic Exhortation, Familiaris consortio, no. 68: A.A.S. 74 (1982), 165.

[30] Cf. C.I.C., can. 1111.

[31] Cf. ibid., can. 1112, '2.

[32] Cf. ibid., can. 1108, '2.

[33] Cf. ibid., can. 1115.

[34] Cf. Second Vatican Council, Constitution on the Sacred Liturgy, Sacrosanctum Concilium, art.78.

[35] Cf. ibid., art. 32.

[36] Cf. Second Vatican Council, Decree on the Apostolate of the Laity, Apostolicam actuositatem, no. 3; Dogmatic Constitution on the Church, Lumen gentium, no. 12.

[37] Cf. C.I.C., can. 844.

[38] Cf. Second Vatican Council, Constitution on the Sacred Liturgy, Sacrosanctum Concilium, art. 37-40 and 63b.

[39] Cf. Second Vatican Council, Constitution on the Sacred Liturgy, Sacrosanctum Concilium, art. 77.

[40] Cf. ibid., art. 78.

[41] Cf. ibid., art. 63b.

[42] Cf. ibid., art. 37.